Reflections of a
Rookie Dean

Reflections of a Rookie Dean

Lessons from the First Year

Prentice T. Chandler
Austin Peay State University

INFORMATION AGE PUBLISHING, INC.
Charlotte, NC • www.infoagepub.com

Library of Congress Cataloging-in-Publication Data

A CIP record for this book is available from the Library of Congress
http://www.loc.gov

ISBN: 978-1-64113-498-9 (Paperback)
978-1-64113-499-6 (Hardcover)
978-1-64113-500-9 (ebook)

Printed in the United States of America

For my wife Kristen, my signal fire.

And my son Silas, my little man.

Contents

Nine Words to Lead By

I don't think I have slept well since August.

The first month I was a dean, I couldn't sleep either. Then one day something hit me, and I've slept like a baby ever since. I was doing the right things whenever I could, I was trusting people, and I was trying my best. Rightness. Trust. Effort. I decided that was probably going to be good enough. It has to be. I decided, in that moment, that we were going to be fine. Leadership is existential. It's a shadow that follows you. Pressing pause and taking a deep breath is a requirement.

(pause)

You are good. You trust. You try. Sleep well. Nine words to lead by.

1

The Challenge of Leadership

The first responsibility of a leader is to define reality. The last is to say thank you.
In between, the leader is a servant.

—Max DuPree

BIG IDEA FOR THIS CHAPTER

This first chapter is an introduction to my past experiences, my leadership philosophy and style, and the nature of change during my first year as dean. I conclude with a section on how this book can be used in leadership development programs.

BIG IDEA

Reflections of a Rookie Dean, pages 1–17
Copyright © 2019 by Information Age Publishing

1

Entering Into a Conversation That's Already Started

Becoming a new dean is like entering into a conversation that's already started. You don't know what was said before you arrived or have a firm grasp on why certain things were said at all. When you become a new dean at a new institution, this idea is even more pronounced. You don't know what was said before you arrived, or why, *and* you don't understand the context of the conversation. Becoming a leader at a new institution and being the outsider is inherently difficult because you are, well, the new person. After a year of serving as a new dean of a college of education, I think the best metaphor to describe this is that you are a *traveler in a foreign land.* The geography, landscapes, culture, pitfalls, personalities, politics, and language are all unknown to you. You are entering into conversations that started before you arrived, you don't understand the context, and you don't quite know the language (yet). You don't quite understand cultural cues, historical context, or ways of interacting with the people you will lead because all of these things were developed, maintained, and reinforced before you arrived. And, with all of this in mind, with your cultural ignorance on full display, you are expected to lead a college. Because you find yourself in a strange land, with strange customs, and a different language, you are going to need direction. The geography/traveler metaphor applies here as well. You are going to need maps, a compass, a guide, and a way to help you understand what you are hearing and seeing. It is my hope that this book serves as that guide for new deans.

The book that you are reading started as a list of ideas. Ideas about leadership that I gleaned from books, advice from other people, personal experience and things I wanted to accomplish. This list became a way for me to organize my thoughts, and it eventually became a way to view how I went about my work. This book can be viewed in several ways. It can be viewed as a running stream of consciousness of my thoughts during my first year as dean. It can also be viewed as advice for incoming or new deans. And, it can be viewed as a compilation of my thoughts on leadership over the past decade of serving in multiple leadership positions in higher education. When I started thinking about being a dean several years ago, I started reading anything I could get my hands on about leadership in higher education. Some of the books I read were general in nature, but most were specifically about leadership as a department chair or dean (more on this in Chapter 2). One of the research findings that appeared over and over in these books was the fact that most leaders at this level come to their positions with no formal training on how to do the job (Gmelch & Buller, 2015). Perhaps this is the way it is, but it doesn't have to be that way. Most of us learn to lead our programs, departments, or colleges through trial and error. In all of my reading and study on how to be an effective leader, I never came across a book written by a rookie dean sharing her/his struggles and reflections. Hopefully this book fills that gap. This book is also for people who are, like I was several years ago, looking for insight into the job of being a dean. Most of the books I read were for people who had already assumed leadership positions in higher education. They were written for people who had already taken positions and were in the process of figuring out how to lead their unit. Hopefully, this book will benefit those of you who are considering college leadership in your future career plans.

As I took my first deanship and began to work with the faculty in my college, people would often point out to me that I ask lots of questions and frame problems for people (or groups of people) out loud. This seemed to be a shift for some of the people with whom I worked. This was an intentional act on my part: the shifting of problem solving from one person (i.e., the leader) to the entire group for consideration. In these situations, I was simply helping people clarify or see problems in a different light so that we, as a group, could own and hopefully solve the problem (Heifetz, 1994). It was in these moments and the conversations that would follow, that faculty would sometimes say, "You should really write a book." Here we are.

Past Experiences Inform the Present

Before assuming my first position as dean, I worked at three other universities and two secondary schools. As an education dean, my experiences are pretty typical—I was a classroom teacher for a number of years, earned a doctorate, became a teacher educator, and worked my way up through the leadership ranks. I started my career in education as a middle school social studies teacher, and during my first year, I was tapped to be the department chair for the social studies department. I was also the school's varsity baseball coach *and* middle school football coach. For those not familiar with rural school districts, new teachers hired into teaching positions are often asked to do a variety of "other jobs" as a part of being a novice teacher. For me, these jobs were department chair, sports coach, yearbook sponsor, among other things. It may seem odd to talk about my first middle school teaching job, but I believe that those experiences as a 21-year-old rookie teacher are applicable to the development of a 38-year-old rookie college dean. The experiences I had as department chair and as a baseball and football coach taught me lessons that I have used throughout my career.

I earned my EdS and PhD degrees while I was teaching, and took my first university position in Alabama in the fall of 2006. The university had three colleges (Arts and Sciences, Business, and Education) with an enrollment of about 3,000 students. My first year as a brand-new assistant professor was not unlike my first year as a middle school teacher/coach. I can still remember the excitement of moving into my new office that summer. As I was bringing boxes of books down the hallway and into my office, I noticed several people doing the opposite. They were moving boxes of books *out* of their offices. These were the faculty members who had retired over the summer and were leaving the university. When I applied for a job at this small teaching university, I was going to be one of four people in the Secondary Education department. Unpacking my office that day, I realized that I would be a department of one. So, by default, once again, I would be the department chair. The learning curve for anyone taking on leadership roles in higher education is steep. Whether you are a new program coordinator, chair, director, or dean there are lots of things that you have to learn and learn quickly. To take on these sorts of roles immediately after the people with the institutional knowledge retire is almost impossible. *Almost.* The first thing I realized in those early days was that the qualitative experience of being a professor did not match what I had imagined. The phone calls and emails never stopped. I was constantly juggling adjunct instructors. I was running searches for faculty line replacements. I was teaching four classes. And, I was finishing my dissertation (I was ABD when I was hired). The lesson I learned that semester was about *structure*. That first semester, I created structures to take care of the small things (phone calls, advising, chain of command) in order for the big things to happen (Chapter 4). I was a Program Chair, Program Coordinator, and Department Chair (name changed with reorganization, but the job stayed the same) for the entire 7 years that I worked at that university.

It was at this university that I learned the basics of how to lead faculty in higher education. I came to the realization pretty quickly that in order to teach my courses (we were on a 4/4 load), advise my students, publish, and build the program, I needed to ensure that the day-to-day operations of the department were on autopilot. This would require that I put certain structures in place to make the operation of the group (once I hired faculty) proactive instead of reactive. In the early days of my time there we lacked any semblance of proactive processes. Instead, we constantly reacted to phone calls, student requests for meetings, and scheduling of courses. We were always responding to things. The world was acting on us—we weren't acting on it. Once those basic structures were in place, the department could focus on bigger, more important things like hiring more faculty, engaging in scholarship, and starting a university center (which we did).

After 7 years in this environment, I applied for and was hired to work at a research intensive (R1) university in Ohio. This position afforded me opportunities and experiences that I simply wouldn't have had at the small school in Alabama. In fact, that is the main reason I decided to look for a job like this. Whereas my first position was at a small, undergraduate teaching institution with very little resources and no national profile, this job was different. I would be working at a research-intensive university with doctoral programs, plenty of resources (comparatively speaking), and a national/international profile in higher education. One of my earliest impressions of this university was that "everything was bigger, better, more." But, for all the bigness of the job and for all of the ways in which this job was different, the leadership dilemmas were largely the same. I would be teaching on a 2/2 load due to the research and scholarly expectations. During my time in Ohio, I would serve in four leadership roles: Coordinator of Social Studies Education, Program Coordinator of Secondary Education (English Language Arts, Mathematics, Science, Social Studies), Interim Program Coordinator of Educational Leadership, and during my last year—Associate Director (AD) of Teacher Education and Leadership. The AD role was created due to a much-needed restructuring in the college and was the first year this position existed. The dilemma of this particular position was that there wasn't precedent to refer to or consult. In this role, I oversaw programs in Curriculum and Instruction, Educational Leadership, Middle Childhood Education, Secondary Education, and Special Education. The experiences I had as the AD of this newly formed unit allowed me to experience leadership on a larger scale than any of my previous positions. In this role, I was overseeing 30 faculty, and I felt that I had a real potential to shape programs and to influence and help faculty develop to their potential.

The biggest issue I had in this new role, and this would also be an issue during my first year as a rookie dean, was that I was working in an environment and with faculty who all (with the exception of three new faculty) had more institutional knowledge than me. This combined with the fact that the position was a new one, made the job especially difficult. Historically, the leadership in this school of education was very decentralized. This new position and the way I envisioned it operating, encroached on this idea and some faculty, predictably, felt threatened. No one likes change. This became clear during my first round of annual reviews and meetings with individual faculty. The process was pretty straightforward. Faculty submitted a yearly report of their accomplishments in scholarship, teaching, and service, and I would meet with the faculty, individually, to discuss the past year. We would talk about strengths and weaknesses in their work, and talk about plans for the next year. The whole process was pretty informal and my write-ups followed a generic template.

One particular review meeting that I had that first year highlights how I frame leadership and the nuances that come with being an externally hired dean. This meeting was with the most senior member of my unit, a full professor who had been at the university for over 30 years. By all accounts, she had done, experienced, and accomplished all there was for a professor in her field to accomplish. She had a reputation of being, depending on who you asked, a great colleague *or* a person that was hard to work with. Since I only had positive experiences with this professor, I viewed her as the former. When she submitted her yearly evaluation to me, she wrote one sentence for each of the three areas (scholarship, teaching, service). By comparison, evaluation statements written by other faculty ranged from 7–15 pages. Frankly, the more that faculty wrote about their accomplishments, the easier it was to conduct the meetings and write their evaluations. They were, in effect, helping me to help them. The more I knew about their work, the better their evaluations tended to go. When we met for her annual performance meeting, I said to her, "I notice that you've provided me very little to go on with respect to your research, teaching, and service. I know that you've done some good work this year, but I need you to fully complete the evaluation form. I need you to help me help you because if I go simply on what you have written here, your evaluation won't be very good." This was my way of explaining to this faculty member that what she submitted would lead to a less than stellar review for that year. In short, I was giving her the benefit of the doubt, and I was trying to help her out. She responded by looking at the document that she had written and said, "None of this matters (pointing to the document) because you can't get rid of me anyways."

At this point, I was confused by her response, and I basically restated what I had just said. She, in turn, repeated herself. I tried to explain that I needed her to fill out the form correctly, so I could adequately write her report. When it became clear that she had no intention of doing so, I made sure that she was aware that my report would only include the three sentences that she wrote. Once I saw that she understood this, I ended the meeting. I wrote the review and sent it up the chain for approvals and signatures.

For about three days, I reflected on what happened in my office that day. In addition to being one of the longest serving professors in the school, I respected this person for her service to the profession. In this exchange with me, she should have served (as I believe our most senior professors should do) as a support and mentor for me, the new leader of the unit. Prior to me taking on the AD role, she and I were cordial with one another and had worked together on accreditation reports. But the meeting we had that day about her evaluation was completely different. The other aspect of that meeting that bothered me was that she did not behave appropriately with me. This professor had, in her career, served in leadership roles, like the one that I now had. She knew from firsthand experience how difficult a job like this can be, and instead of being supportive (as she was in my previous encounters) she was downright hostile to me. After a couple days of thinking about this meeting, I decided to go to her and talk about what happened during her evaluation. My reasoning was simple: if I allowed this sort of behavior in my role as the AD, I would be setting a precedent for future behavior. I walked down to her office and knocked on her office door.

"Can I talk to you for a minute?"

"Sure. What's up?"

"I'd like to talk with you about our evaluation meeting the other day." At this point, her demeanor changed and she turned away from her computer to face me. I continued,

"I think that the way you talked to me the other day about your evaluation was unacceptable. I was simply asking you to do what you know that you are required to do. I am not trying to get rid of you. I am still confused as to why you would make the leap that I am trying to get rid of you when all I asked you to do was to complete your evaluation form, just like you have every other year that you have worked here. I thought that I could count on your support in this new role. When I took this job, you congratulated me, and told me that I could come to you for advice. You know how hard a job like this can be. You are putting me in a difficult situation over something as simple as this. I don't like it."

"Well, you can't get rid of me."

"I am not trying to get rid of you. You are one of the most accomplished people in our school. I honor and respect your service to this University. Why on earth would you think that I am trying to get rid of you?"

The conversation turned to her apologizing to me and explaining her recent history with upper administration. She believed she was being targeted, and told me a couple stories to back up her beliefs. Her response to me that day during the evaluation meeting, although it wasn't professional, was a response framed by her struggles and experiences with people in charge. Here's the point in telling this story: *I had no idea about any of this.* Our encounter was framed by events that I couldn't have possibly known about. We were viewing this meeting from completely different standpoints. For her, the meeting was a continuation of the mistreatment she was suffering from administration. Since I was the new administrator in the role, I was guilty by association. That was her frame of reference. It wasn't true, accurate, or fair, but that's how she saw our encounter. For me, the meeting was the first evaluation meeting between me and one of the few full professors in the college. It was stressful because I was going to have to have a difficult conversation with someone that I respected. My goal was not to "get rid of her." Quite the contrary, I simply wanted her to comply with the evaluation protocol. It was interesting to see the tone of voice soften and the temperature in the room decrease as we talked that day. I told her that I was in leadership because I like to help people do good things, not to lord over people and fire them (which I had no authority to do anyway). The next morning, she submitted her revised evaluation form. This story reveals a larger lesson that came out in several instances in my first year as a rookie dean. *There is always a backstory.* This professor had a backstory, and that narrative framed her encounter with me. The way she framed me, and the way that she framed our meeting is less about fairness and more about acknowledging that when you are in leadership, you are already thought of in certain ways by certain people. In my first year as a dean, I had to remind myself of this on a regular basis. In fact, the more "powerful" your title and the more symbolic power people ascribe to you, they assign intention to your actions, whether it matches your true intentions or not.

First Things First

You only get one chance to make a first impression, so goes the saying. For new leaders, this moment comes the first time that you speak with your faculty. Being a new dean in a new university, I knew that I wanted to make a good impression during the first faculty meeting of the year. Because I knew that there were lots of things I did not know about this new university, I decided to have short meetings with my leadership team to plan college-wide meetings. I decided to have this first pre-meeting as another layer of support for the first full faculty gathering. It worked so well, that I decided to make this a part of the way we did business in the college. The advice, support, and guidance from my leadership team in helping me think through issues *before* college meetings was one of the best decisions I made during my first year as dean.

During our first faculty meeting of the year, I wanted to give the faculty an idea of who I was as a leader. I was replacing a dean with over 30 years of experience at this institution, so there would be (as I anticipated) a cultural shift in the ways people viewed the office of dean within the college. The sketch I provide below is how I thought about and presented myself to the college. It is intended to help new deans think about how they frame themselves, and, equally as important, to think about how others frame them as well. This section also alludes to and foreshadows some of the themes that we will see later in the book, although I couldn't have known it during that first meeting.

My Leadership Philosophy

One of my default positions is that if you have hardworking, talented people in the right positions, your job as a leader is much easier. This much is clear. If you don't have the right people in the right positions, you have a couple options: you can try to find the right people for your team or you can "coach up" the people you have in place and try and help them get better at the things they struggle with. I prefer the latter. We are all good at some things and not so good at others. *I believe that a dean's primary role is to create conditions where people can do good work.* When I say conditions, the two words that come to mind are "positive" and "productive." Anything I can do to make sure that this sort of environment is established and nurtured, I will do. I have several corollaries that correspond to this overarching idea.

> If there is a better way to do it, we should do it that way.
> We should simplify our environment (i.e., systems) when we can.
> Trust people to do the job.
> Leaders don't create followers; leaders create more leaders.

That is leadership at the dean level. Adhering to these simple principles is the reason, I believe, that we had a successful first year as a college with a rookie dean. Part of the "creating conditions" is removing the things that stop us from doing good work. An aspect of this idea is additive, where we *add to* the way we do and think about things. The other part (and I think this isn't as common) is subtractive in nature. We in higher education are really good at adding things to the menu of tasks that faculty and staff attend to on a daily basis. Sometimes we need to let things go. Completely. We are so used to carrying unnecessary tasks around with us that we don't notice the cumulative weight of things that aren't integral to the jobs we do. We need to get in the habit of letting go of things that don't support our work. As the dean, I want to make sure that I am helping people let go of unnecessary parts of their work as faculty and staff. During our meeting, I used an image to make this point. This image was a derivation of Sisyphus, the character from Greek mythology that was forced by the gods to roll an immense boulder up a hill, only to have it roll back down on him for all of eternity. In this image, there was an added feature. Sisyphus has *another boulder* chained to his leg. For me, in this setting, this image was perfect. The boulder represented the jobs we all have in higher education. It can be difficult work that sometimes seems insurmountable. One of the jobs that I have as a dean is to do something about the *other* boulder around your leg. This represents the things we should let go of and be freed from its weight. As dean, I want to focus on that extra weight and do whatever I can to get rid of it.

In my first meeting, I also talked briefly about the concept of "Positive Academic Leadership" (Buller, 2013). Positive Academic Leadership, among other things, emphasizes people's strengths, seeks to be proactive, and is people oriented. When people apply for positions in higher education in leadership, they often talk about their leadership style. Positive Academic Leadership is a school of thought that closely aligns with the way that I see my role as dean. I view this idea as a framework that helps me think about how to go about leading the college on a day-to-day basis. But, discussing leadership in this way can come across as too academic or that I am simply borrowing ideas from other people (which was the case). So, during my first talk to the faculty I had two other slides that focused more on the leader that I was and hoped to be in my time as dean. I think that these two ideas will also give the reader a glimpse into the way that I think about leading change and leading people in the college.

The first idea is the difference between "practical" leadership and "visionary" leadership. Perhaps this separation is arbitrary, but it helps me think through what types of strategies and mindsets to bring to my work. Practical leadership is simply "how we do things around here." This isn't particularly exciting or inspirational and can be pretty mundane stuff. I believe, however, that these things must be taken care of before visionary leadership can occur. The practical part is the structures that we have in place so we aren't always reacting to our environment. Workload forms. Orientations. Advising protocols. Travel request. Workflow of forms through the dean's office. All of these mundane tasks take us away from the big work that we are all hired to do. The big work is the visionary leadership piece. These are the big picture goals for the college. You can, as a group, accomplish big goals, but it's much harder if you are constantly struggling to accomplish the small day-to-day task simultaneously. As the new dean, my big picture goals were to support more scholarship and grant writing, improve our partnerships with schools, create a minority faculty association, and establish our first doctoral program.

The other thing that I discussed with my faculty at our first meeting was a slide titled "The New Guy." This was my non-academic way of attempting to describe my leadership style to the people I would be leading. Since I started my post as dean on July 1st and our meeting was in mid-August, I was able to see how the college operated before I spoke to the faculty for the first time. This allowed me some context from which to think about how I would fit within the existing college culture. Below is a partial list of the items that I discussed:

1. **That's not the way we do that:** I had heard this stated numerous times in my first month. I wanted the faculty to know that I was open to new ways of doing things. In areas where things were working, we'd remain steady. In areas where we needed to improve we would evolve.
2. **We can do it fast, or we can do it right:** I prefer doing a few things well (i.e., quality) rather than many things poorly and fast. In my first month there seemed to be a rush to do everything, right now. I wanted to change that mindset. Let's slow down and do it right.
3. **Assume positive intent:** In my interactions with faculty, I assume positive intent. I give people the benefit of the doubt until proven otherwise. Since this is my default position for faculty, it is also useful if faculty assume positive intent when it comes to my decisions as the dean. This is a two-way street. I made this an explicit request in my remarks. We are all better off when we give the other person the benefit of the doubt.
4. **Stop emails:** I am a supporter of a healthy work–life balance, whenever possible. Under normal circumstances, I will not email after 5:00 p.m. or on the weekends.
5. **Communication style:** I have an open and direct communication style. If there are decisions or issues that concern you, please come and talk to me. It's okay to disagree with me.
6. **Chain of command:** I support faculty going through their chairs to the dean's office. I support students going through their professors and their department chairs before they come to the dean's office.
7. **Proactive:** I prefer being proactive to being reactive. In fact, leading from a reactive stance is not a strong suit of mine.

Change and Being the New Guy

Man who says it cannot be done should not interrupt man doing it.
—Confucius

The months leading up to my first dean's job, I made lists. Lots of lists. These lists ranged from practical things I'd like to do as a dean to ensure efficiencies in a college to ideas for publications to more global ideas like starting academic centers and new degree programs. Usually an idea or a thought would hit me during times when I wasn't trying to think of new ideas. This phenomenon is backed by science. We often get our best ideas and greatest insights when we are in the shower or going for an afternoon jog or while cooking dinner. When our mind is on autopilot, we seem to have a knack for good ideas. As I was wrapping up my job at one university and planning to start a new job at a different school in a different state with a different title, the lists became longer and longer. The irony of these lists of great ideas is that I was planning to change/fix things that I didn't know were problems (yet).

When I would meet colleagues at other universities who were already deans, I would ask them for their advice. Much of their advice sounded like common sense, and the most common piece of advice I was given was to pace myself and not make too many changes at the beginning. The idea was simple. Go in to your new job, spend some time getting to know how things work, take it all in, understand the issues, and then, and only then, should I act. During my first year, I was able to put this advice into action for most issues that the college faced. It turns out that most of the issues that I faced as a first year dean were not huge, catastrophic problems. They were issues or problems that had developed over time that most of the faculty, because of their gradual development, didn't perceive as a big deal. Faculty members in the college were simply unaware that some of the things they did, on a practical level, were inefficient or outdated. This has been the case in every job I have had. That doesn't make them bad faculty or people, it just means that they had been doing things a certain way for so long that it seemed natural and common sense. One of the dangers of common sense is that when it becomes ingrained in the way people see the world it takes on the nature of being an unquestionable truth. We are all guilty of this in certain aspects of our lives. Framing things as common sense is our (human) way of simplifying the worlds that we inhabit. The problem arises when we question the long-standing or traditional ways of doing things.

Another piece of advice that I picked up before I took the job as dean was to frame my deanship not simply as replacing their ways of doing things, but rather building upon the traditions and positive things they were already doing. At first glance, this seems like advice to manipulate people, but it isn't. There are things that will have to be replaced. But those things are usually rare. It is rare that we have a complete replacement of a system within a college by a first-year dean. I think they are rare because this is (1) difficult to do and (2) first-year deans don't have enough information to make this sort of change. What we usually wind up doing instead of wholesale replacement of protocols and systems is that we *reform* things that need to be improved (read that "re"-"form"). We take systems that are not as efficient as they could be, we see them with a new eye, we apply our own frames of reference (from past experiences), we suggest changes, and reform it. To simply say that you are going to do away with a system that's been in place sends the message that everyone was doing it wrong before you arrived to set them straight. This is something that you should say to your new faculty, and you should say it often. This idea—the idea of improving systems and efficiencies—was one of the things I talked about at our very first faculty meeting. We remember the first things and the last things that people say to us. I made it a point to say this during the first part of our first faculty meeting because I realize how important this concept is. I also reiterated it during every faculty meeting that we had that year: "I am not *replacing* your ways of doing things. We are making improvements and adjustments to improve how we serve our students."

During my first year as dean I noticed something that I had seen at my other university jobs. When I discovered a system or way of doing things that didn't quite work as well as it should, I found that the people in these systems were all the same in one respect. They were all well-intentioned, hardworking, smart people who were reacting to ill-fitting and inefficient systems, systems that had evolved over time to fit personalities, preferences, and mindsets, rather than the needs of the organization. This was a secondary message that I reiterated to my faculty that first year. The point was that even though we are changing the way we do some things in the college, it isn't personal. In reality, the fact that they have been able to function as well as they have with a reactive, inefficient system is a testament to the work ethic, patience, and effort of the people working within the system. This is less about attacking the ways that things are done and more about finding ways that are smarter, not harder. I know this sounds cliché, but it's really that simple. In fact, some faculty have done things a certain way for so long that they simply can't imagine another way of doing things. There were several times during my first year where I could actually see this look on people's faces. It was like you were saying something that they didn't understand, and perhaps they didn't. Or at least they didn't in the moment. This moment was usually followed by a statement of how it was done in the past and how the "new way" wouldn't work. In fact, many of these responses were personal in nature. I had, in very subtle ways, offended their sensibilities about the way they had conducted business before I arrived. And usually the bigger the change you want to make, the more personal it becomes.

How to Use This Book

Before we move to the lessons that I learned during my first year, I'd like to say a word about how to use the chapters and ideas that follow. Conceptually, the ideas that are in the following chapters can be used in a variety of ways. I envision that most people will use this book in much the same way that I used books about leadership when I was planning to become a dean. Most will read it for insight into the job of being a dean with the hopes that something I say will help them to prepare for their future leadership roles. This is my sincere hope as well. A second avenue for the book is to serve as a text in university programs directed towards internal capacity building. This would include program directors, department chairs, associate directors, or professors who are thinking about a career in higher education leadership. Many universities have internal programs designed to train future administrators within their current ranks of professors. This book can be used as a resource for colleges and universities to build their own leadership capacities in these programs (Gmelch, Hopkins, & Damico, 2011). For example, Central Michigan University has an "Administrative Fellows Program" whose stated purpose is to offer "professional development opportunities for tenured faculty members at the University to further develop leadership skills, to become more effective in their current positions, and to intensively explore an interest in becoming administrative leaders in the future" (Central Michigan University, 2017). A third purpose of this book is to serve as a text for university courses in higher educational administration. Graduate programs in higher education could benefit from texts that look at the experiences (successes and failures) of novice deans in their first positions.

When I became dean, I established a "Dean's Council" to serve as the college leadership team (Chapter 3). I imagine this book being used in these settings as well, to help college leaders think through and wrestle with leadership dilemmas. Furthermore, I believe that much of what I have to say in the pages that follow are applicable to most leadership situations and contexts. Although I am writing about the higher education context specifically, the ideas in this book have served me as a classroom teacher, a sports coach, a department chair, a director, and now as a college dean. The thinkers who have influenced my thinking on a range of issues related to leadership come from a variety of fields, including business, technology, psychology, history, philosophy, and the military. These ideas have changed the way I think about my leadership in higher education, and I hope that what I share gives you insight into the type of leader you will be. Many aspects of experiencing leadership, from the vantage point of a leader, are open ended. It has multiple points of view, possible solutions, and diversity of personality. The art of leadership lies in noticing and embracing this variety and diversity of thought.

Before we leave Chapter 1, I'd like to set the stage for the rest of the book by noting several themes that run throughout the chapters that follow. These themes are *people first, change is the only constant, process is everything,* and *gratitude.* I believe that most of these ideas are implied by what I have to say about my first-year experiences, but just in case they aren't clear, here they are. I know there is danger in writing about college leadership after only one year of experience, but I am ok with that. Is there a possibility that I have written something that turns out to be naive or misguided? Maybe. Are there things that I missed or unintentionally misrepresented? Probably. But, that's not the point of this book. This book is about sharing my impressions during my first year as a dean—in the hopes that people can learn from my experiences. Mistakes and misperceptions are mine alone.

People First

During my year as dean, it was immediately clear that this job is about people. Working with people. Taking care of people. Supporting people. Teaching and learning from people. Succeeding and failing with people. We don't do this job disconnected and separated from other human beings. We do it together. Never forget that. When you put people first, you set the stage for great things to happen.

Change is the Only Constant

Much of what I have to say about my first year as dean involves change. *And, this is how it's supposed to work.* When a college gets new leadership, there are going to be changes. In every job I've had in education, I have had new principals, deans, provosts, and presidents change some aspect of the way things worked. It wasn't always popular change, but it came all the same. Change should not be viewed as a negative commentary on the people who came before us. It should not be viewed as a criticism of the ways that other people attempted to do your job. We do things in different ways to fit the way we see a situation (or problem). Change is always context based and is viewed through our personal problem-solving lens. What works for one leader, doesn't work for another. Things that I do as the leader of this college will, one day, be changed by the person who follows me. That's normal. Even with all of the changes we made this first year, we weren't really *replacing* so much as we were *building upon* the good work that people were doing before I arrived. The operation of a good college is cumulative in nature. Intellectual capital and experience builds over the years, accumulating to give us the institutions we know and love today. After all, there were people doing great things before I arrived, and they will be doing great things after I am gone. Because change allows it.

Process is Everything

There were no moments of sudden, earth changing transformation. There were no "ah ha" moments that suddenly turned the operations of the college into a well-oiled machine. In the stories that we tell ourselves, this narrative often dominates. Those fleeting moments when everything changes (for good or bad). Except that's not how it really works. The "ah ha" moments, instead of creating instantaneous change, served to start the ball rolling on the *incremental* changes that we decided to make. During my first year, the great things we were able to do were the result of planning, collaboration, hard work, and following a process. Sometimes a slow and arduous process. Be patient because great things don't happen overnight. Being a dean and being a leader are processes. It's something that you develop into, it's not something that you are or aren't. It's something that you become.

Gratitude

I am thankful for the experiences I had during my first year as dean. I was able to work with talented staff, faculty, and administrators doing important and meaningful work. I am thankful for the faculty and college dean who came before me, who set the stage for my successes. I am thankful for the patience and grace that was extended to me by the university community as I learned how to be a college leader. I am fully aware, that as the dean of the college, I stand on the shoulders of those that came before me. Their work is now my work. And, I am thankful to be the next link in the chain of the work we are all here to do.

References

Buller, J. L. (2013). *Positive academic leadership: How to stop putting out fires and start Making a difference.* San Francisco, CA: Jossey-Bass.

Central Michigan University (2017). *Administrative Fellows Program* [PDF file]. Retrieved from https://www.cmich.edu/office_president/Documents/Administrative%20Fellows.pdf

Gmelch, W., & Buller, J. (2015). *Building academic leadership capacity: A guide to best practices.* San Francisco, CA: Jossey-Bass.

Gmelch, W., Hopkins, D., & Damico, S. (2011). *Seasons of a dean's life: Understanding the role and building leadership capacity.* Sterling, VA: Stylus.

Heifetz, R. (1994*). Leadership without easy answers.* Cambridge, MA: Harvard University Press.

2

Be a Student of Leadership

Education is the mother of leadership.
—Wendell Willkie

BIG IDEA

BIG IDEA FOR THIS CHAPTER

In my first year, I found it very helpful to read, study, and become a student of leadership. In this chapter I share three ideas—framing, adaptive leadership, and voice—that helped me think about my role as a rookie dean. For new leaders, diversity of thought in the ways we think about our roles is a good thing. It helps us to see the world through multiple lenses and develop solutions that we wouldn't have thought of before. This chapter is a bit more academic than the other chapters, but it serves to set the stage for the experiences I write about later. It includes lists of resources that can support your learning as well.

One of the stated goals of a liberal arts education is that graduates will go on to be "lifelong learners,"—the idea that what you know is as important as how you know. With the exception of people who have earned degrees in higher education administration the overwhelming majority of people who become deans have degrees in a field unrelated to the task of academic leadership. When I was thinking of becoming a dean about five years ago, I talked to as many people as I could to get their advice and suggestions. Some of the people that I spoke to were faculty, some were department chairs, and a few were deans. The advice that I got most often was to "never stop learning." I talked with my mentor about the move from faculty to administration often in the years leading up to my first dean job. I met her when I was at my first university job in Alabama. She has experiences at several universities over the course of her career and has been a successful teacher, scholar, and leader for the better part of 40 years. I began to seriously think about becoming a dean when I was in Ohio. When I began talking to her about this career shift, I can vividly remember our conversation. I asked her, "Where do I start? I have been a teacher and a professor for a decade... how do you make this transition?" Her answer was automatic. "You should talk to as many people as possible. And, you should read everything you can get your hands on about being a dean."

So that's what I did. I sought out people who were already school leaders and I picked their brains for ideas. Since I was at a university that had plenty of professional development opportunities, I sought out and participated in programs and conferences directed towards academic leadership. I read as many books as I could find on being a successful chair, dean, and provost. I reasoned that if I wanted to be a leader, I still had lots to learn. I became a dean in the fall of 2017, my twelfth year in higher education. And, although I had been a department chair or program coordinator for my entire career, the things I knew and the things I had learned were mostly from implementing the trial and error method. In those jobs, I was thrust into leadership roles with no training or preparation for how to lead an academic unit, and I had to figure it out. When I eventually became a dean, I did not want that same experience.

Viewing Problems Through a Frame

How we approach problems is determined by many things. Oftentimes we look at issues and problems through our personal experiences with similar situations. We take a look at a problem and we try to solve it by applying a solution that worked in another setting or context. The good news is that this works most of the time, particularly with problems that arise in the context of a program, department, or unit within a college. The language and the landscape of the problem are often similar, and so the strategies and ideas that we bring to the problem are often interchangeable. This line of thinking, although logical and effective most of the time, prevents us from seeing different types of problems, well, differently. I have found in my experience that applying the same lenses to all problems prevents me from seeing what I need to see in order to arrive at a solution. Sometimes I have made problems worse because I am applying a frame of reference to the problem that doesn't fit. The other problem that is caused when we view all problems the same is that we fail to take advantage of the opportunity to learn and to give the work back to the people (Heifetz, 1994).

In the summer of 2016, I was fortunate to participate in the Management Development Program (MDP) in the Graduate School of Education at Harvard University. This program was developed for educational leaders with 7–10 years of experience at the coordinator, chair, director, associate dean, and dean levels. It was a 2-week, intensive institute devoted, in part, to helping leaders see problems in different and nuanced ways. The curriculum used case studies to help us all look at educational problems from multiple points of view. We had guest speakers that were former and current university presidents. The cohort had 100 participants and we were organized into small working groups. When the whole class met, we would grapple with case studies from higher education and listen to a variety of speakers who represented educational leadership from around the country. In the small group settings, we were able to take the information from our class sessions and readings and apply them to actual problems that we (the small group participants) were having at our respective institutions. Each team member would bring an issue to the group, and it was our task to problem solve. Since this was the summer before I took on the newly created associate director role, the problem I brought to the team was one of context, structure, and organizational legitimacy in my new job.

Learning from my classmates at MDP was one of the most formative experiences of my professional and educational career. The main text for the MDP was the classic leadership text, *Reframing Organizations: Artistry, Choice, and Leadership* by Lee Bolman and Terrence Deal (2013). In their work, the authors discuss how we can frame problems within our organization as belonging to one of four frames: structural, human resources, political, and symbolic. These four frames serve as metaphors for examining your organization (or in our case, college/university) and the issues, challenges, and problems that you face as a leader. Each frame has central concepts, images, and challenges. The structural frame examines how the organization is designed: organizational concepts, rules, policies, chain of command, protocols. The human resource frame delves into the human side of the people in our organizations: their strengths and weaknesses, what makes them tick, their emotions, thoughts, and attachments to the work they are doing. The political frame enters into the exercise of power within the organization: competition, struggles for resources and recognition, control of the environment. Lastly, the symbolic frame focuses on how people make meaning of their organization: the culture, myths, and stories that we tell to give our organization meaning (Bolman & Deal, 2013, p. 19).

The main take away for me, as a rookie dean, is that this framework helps me to think about problems in a more complex way. I realize that to say that this framework allows me to think about problems in a "more complex" way sounds counter-intuitive. Don't we want our problems to be less complex? For me, this framework allows me, almost forces me to look at problems, all problems, for what they represent. Not all problems are the same, which means that not all solutions to problems should be the same. Certain kinds of problems require certain kinds of solutions. As the authors explain:

> it can be liberating to realize there is always more than one way to respond to any problem or dilemma. Those who master reframing report a sense of choice and power. Managers are imprisoned only to the extent that their palette of ideas is impoverished. (Bolman & Deal, 2013, p. 19)

Every idea that we have about how a problem might be solved is only a partial solution. No matter the solution (or the ideas that you bring to bear on a problem) there is always a blind spot. For me, this is the beauty of using this idea to frame my work as a leader. There are very few perfect solutions to complicated problems. As leaders we are tasked with finding solutions to problems and realize, along the way, that these solutions are imperfect by their very nature. There is saying in social science that for every complicated, social/human problem, there is a very clear and simple solution that is almost always wrong. Complex organizations with complex problems by their very nature have complex solutions, not simple ones. The goal as a leader is not to solve every problem once and for all in one fell swoop. It is to first recognize the nature of problems, their possible solutions, and apply these solutions appropriately to the issues that you face. In looking at problems in a more honest and realistic way, we are relieving the pressure to solve everything right now, once and for all. These frames serve as "filters for sorting essence from trivia, maps that aid navigation, and tools for solving problems and getting things done" (Bolman & Deal, 2013, p. 21).

During my time at Harvard, the organizers gave us a "cheat sheet" that helped us think through though the four frames (see Figure 2.1). When

HARVARD
GRADUATE SCHOOL of EDUCATION
Harvard Institutes for Higher Education

MANAGEMENT
DEVELOPMENT PROGRAM
JUNE 5 – 17, 2016

A Four Frames Cheat Sheet

Structural

Organization Chart
Rationality
Measureable Objectives
Division of Labor
Coordination and control

Restructuring
Rules, policies, and procedures
Clarity of roles and responsibilities
Chain of Command
Formal/official authority

Human Resource

Motivation and engagement
Human needs
Fit between people and organization
Nurturing, personal growth, fostering
    individual capabilities
Training, learning, and professional
    development

Inclusion and participation
Feedback for improvement
Emotional intelligence
Autonomy and empowerment
Participation

Political

Power, exercised in multiple ways
Scarce resources
Enduring differences
Coalitions, stakeholders, alliances, interest
    Groups
Bargaining

Negotiation
Interests/Currencies of exchange
Networking
Influence, with or without formal authority
Authorizing environment

Symbolic

Meanings and interpretations
Culture
Ceremony
Vision
Storytellling

Inspire by example
Celebrations and heroes
Explain and reassure through ritual
"Brand"

Figure 2.1   A four frames cheat sheet.

I took on my job as the new associate director and one year later when I became a dean, this sheet was never far away. When confronted with a problem, take the time to determine what sort of problem it is. Determining the nature of a problem will help you determine the types of solutions and strategies that you bring to the table. One of the most eye-opening activities that we did during the MDP experience was to determine which of the frames that we, as leaders, gravitate towards. Of the four frames, we all have one that we tend to have a strength in, or that we seem to use more often than the others. It is interesting to discover that you see problems through a specific "default" lens. If you are always seeing problems through the political lens, you are missing out on helping your team to solve structural, human resource, and/or symbolic problems. In trying to help our teams solve problems we want to make sure that we are bringing the right tools, mindsets, and strategies to the job. For me, it was interesting to discover my default frames when trying to solve problems. It allowed me to see how I approach problem solving and alerted me to the things I am probably missing. When confronted with a problem in your organization, ask yourself, "What frame fits this problem?" The answer to this question, although it won't immediately solve your issue, will point you in the right direction.

In my experiences, my default frame is almost always structural in nature. I am looking for a solution to a problem that lies in the way the problem is organized. Are our rules and procedures clear? Do we have a policy for that? Would this work better if this part were over here? Who has the authority in this situation? This frame and these questions have served me well in my career as an educational leader and in my first year as a dean. But, this frame is only as useful as the problem to which it's being applied. The structural frame isn't as useful for a non-structural problem. In fact, it can be counterproductive if there is a major misfit between the problem and the frame. A human resource dilemma (involving emotion and attachments to the workplace) is rarely solved by only looking at the structure of an organization. Our solution should align with our problem. Different problems require different solutions, and more importantly, they require different mindsets. The art of applying frames is ensuring that the frame that you are applying matches the type of problem before you.

When I became dean, one of the first things that I did was to create a "Dean's Council" (Chapter 3). This group of people included the associate dean, the two department chairs, the director of teacher education, the licensure officer, and my most senior staff member. The stated goal of this group was to help me think about the college from a global perspective. We met once a month to discuss a topic or theme, and to have conversations about how we, as a group of leaders, can make the college better. At our first meeting of the year, we discussed Bolman and Deal's (2013) Four Frames and the "cheat sheet." I gave each member of the Dean's Council a copy of *Reframing Academic Leadership* (2011) written by Lee Bolman and Joan Gallos. This book utilizes the ideas in Reframing Organizations and places them in the context of colleges and universities. The authors remind us "a central mistake that leaders in any context is to lock into limited and flawed views of their world" (p. 23). During our regularly scheduled meetings and for times when we were meeting separately to think about issues, our starting point was first to determine what kind of problem or issue was before us. I like to think of using the four frames as a toolbox. The toolbox metaphor fits here because when we use a toolbox, we are selecting a specific tool for specific task or job. If the only tool you have is a hammer, then we begin to treat everything as if it were a nail (Maslow, 1966). By thinking of the frames as tools that can be used for specific tasks, we broaden our repertoire for managing and solving problems.

Structural

This could be anything in your organization that deals with how people are organized, the rules and policies that you have in place, and how tasks are divided among and between people. Example: A new dean may want to ensure that all programs within a college have standard program handbooks for incoming students. This would provide structure and continuity for students and their faculty advisers in terms of course content, requirements, and common information that are applicable to all students within a program.

Human Resource

Problems that fall into this category deal with human needs, motivation, and how people within the organization connect with one another. Example: Most universities are attuned to the issue of a lack of representation of people of color among the students and faculty. This is especially acute when it comes to the recruitment and retention of faculty in nearly every type of college. In my experiences across three universities, there is recognition that this is a problem, followed by a lack of action. A new dean could support the creation of a Minority Faculty Association to focus exclusively on the recruitment and retention of more people of color to the faculty ranks.

Political

This frame examines problems that deal with the exercise of power. Politics involves the mechanism by which people get resources, how decisions are made, and how community members perceive influence. Example: In my experiences, power is displayed most obviously in college meetings, in which the leader of the group (i.e., the dean) does most of the talking, directs others to talk, and announces major decisions that have been made. A new dean may want to flip this script to ensure that power is exercised by multiple people/factions within the college. This can be accomplished in the context of faculty meetings. What would a college wide meeting look like if the majority of your faculty participated in the meeting (i.e., not just listen to decisions that have already been made)?

Symbolic

Symbolic problems are tied to meanings that flourish (or don't) within an organization. What is the vision/culture/story of your college? What is your college about? Example: Within colleges of education, there are moments that serve as rites of passage for students progressing through a program. One of the most important is the moment that students move from their coursework to the internship portion of their program. A new dean might institute a formal ceremony where this rite of passage moment is recognized for the important day that it is. It formalizes the meaning through ceremony and thus becomes a ritual to which the college and our interns assign meaning. During my first year as a dean, we instituted just such a ceremony where interns were given a lapel pin with the college seal on it. This represents symbolic meaning to our students and the pin serves as an outward representation to the world that they are part of our tribe.

What Does it Mean to Adapt?

Another idea that helped me during my first year as dean was Ronald Heifetz's notion of adaptive leadership (Heifetz, 1994). I find this idea attractive because it allows leaders to evolve, flex, bend, and adapt to the context of a problem. Oftentimes we think of leaders as being rigidly stubborn people who stick to a particular position, and through sheer force of will, accomplish the goals of the organization. In my experiences, people like this aren't very successful as leaders in higher education. It's not because they don't get things done necessarily—many times they do get things done. But, it's in how they get the job done and the toll that it takes on people that becomes the problem. As was the case with thinking about problems through frames, adaptive leadership asks us to think about problems and the types of work that will ultimately lead to a solution. Not all problems are the same and therefore, not all solutions are equal.

In this framework there are three kinds of problems (Heifetz, Grashow, & Linsky, 2009, p. 20).

> **Type 1:** A clear problem with a clear solution that falls to the leader to solve. These problems require a technical solution.

Example: The semester schedule was submitted in a variety of ways by the chairs and the program coordinators. I have experienced this issue at every university I have served. The schedule is due on a certain date or time window, and the person responsible for the schedule submits the information in a way that's different from other people working on the schedule. A secondary problem with submitting the schedule is the issue of timing. I wanted the schedule submitted with a buffer of time between submission to me and the time when it was submitted to the registrar. As the chair or the dean, this is a clear problem with a technical solution. I required that everyone working on the schedule submit their portion of the schedule in an: (1) electronic template within a specific (2) time frame that allowed for review and corrections before the "final draft" was entered into the system for processing.

Type 2: A clear problem that requires learning in which the leader takes the lead in directing the group towards a solution. These problems require a mix of technical and adaptive solutions.

Example: In colleges of education, we are required to monitor the professional dispositions of the people going through our programs. Every program in the country is required by accrediting bodies to evaluate whether or not the people who complete our programs have the dispositions required of the profession of teaching. This includes traits like collaboration, positive attitude, communication skills, initiative, and respect for diversity. If a student fails to meet the dispositions of the program during their time in the field, there should be a process for helping the student to remediate their dispositions or to be counseled out of the program. A lack of process and protocol to deal with this is a problem. This is a clear problem requiring a mix of technical and adaptive solutions. In this case, it is the leader's responsibility to make it clear that a process is needed and to collaboratively develop a protocol to handle situations where students do not exhibit appropriate behavior or dispositions. In the past, I have (as the chair or dean) provided technical assistance with this problem in the form of providing examples (i.e., creating a "Professional Review Board") from my previous jobs in other colleges of education. The adaptive work commences when the department or college commits to learning about these structures and develops one to fit the needs of their current situation.

Type 3: An unclear problem that requires learning in which the group takes the lead in owning the problem and committing themselves to solving the problem. These problems require adaptive work in which the group learns new ways of framing problems.

Example: A large part of what colleges of education do involves collaboration. We collaborate with other colleges to ensure that our students receive appropriate core/general education courses. We collaborate with arts and sciences to ensure that our teachers have the requisite content knowledge to teach required subjects in public schools. We collaborate with the agencies at the state and federal level to ensure we are meeting current regulations and guidelines. We collaborate with our accrediting bodies to ensure that we are meeting the latest iteration of standards that lead to effective teachers in every classroom. Most importantly, we collaborate with local school districts for the placement of our students for clinical placements and teaching internships. It is not uncommon for these collaborations/relationships to be strained over time. The reason is simple. Both sides are busy working their side of the equation: schools are in the business of educating children, colleges are in the business of educating future teachers and meeting state, federal, and accreditation standards.

Ideally, the relationship between a college of education and a local school district should represent a true partnership in which the responsibility for the education of teachers is shared between colleges of education and the school district. To do otherwise ignores the practical expertise that exists in schools. Given the many moving parts in this relationship, it is not uncommon for faculty in colleges of education and teachers/administrators in local schools to be unclear on the issues that need to be resolved to repair and improve these relationships. This represents an unclear problem that requires learning in which the group takes the lead in owning the problem and committing themselves to solving the problem. This will involve the groups involved meeting to clearly define the problem, listen to one another, learn to see the education of teachers as a truly collaborative activity, and commit to changing our attitudes and practices. This is hard work that will only be successful to the extent that the sides are willing to compromise and learn from one another in the process.

The examples that I have laid out—course scheduling, protocols to ensure professional dispositions, and relationships with local schools—are admittedly mundane in their scope. But, it is the ordinary, routine parts of our organizations that need to be as clear and efficient as possible. Without clear methods for resolving these issues, we are left with the following outcomes:

- A course schedule that does not meet the needs of students
- An intern teaching children who does not possess the mindsets and dispositions required of a teacher
- A dysfunctional relationship with the local school district

A constant part of my leadership responsibilities wherever I have worked is to ensure that systems work, that the small things that are necessary to run an organization (no matter how large or small) get done. But, there are also the big things that must get accomplished as well—grants, accreditation, hiring new faculty, starting new programs. The two ways of seeing and solving problems that I have sketched out, framing and adaptive leadership, allow us to determine the nature of the problem so we can more quickly get to the nature of the solution. In my experience as a first-year dean, this mindset served me well. Simply start by asking yourself,

- What kind of problem is this? (structural, human resource, political, or symbolic)
- Is this a technical problem in which you can provide a ready-made, time tested solution or is it adaptive, one in which you and your faculty will need to learn new ways of doing things?

Voice

Another resource that I have found very useful during my first year as dean has been articles from the Harvard Business Review. I follow HBR on social media, and have access to their small, succinct articles on leadership. They are perfect because they are short reads that you can fit in to your busy day. They are also great to send to your leadership team as common reading material for the group to consider. One of my favorites is an article by Su titled, "You Don't Just Need One Leadership Voice—You Need Many." Amy Jen Su writes about the ways in which your voice as a leader varies depending on the context and situation.

> We often equate developing a leadership voice with finding ways to appear more confident. We assume that our success depends upon mimicking someone else, increasing self-promotion, or saying things louder than others. But rather than living with imposter's syndrome, or feeling exhausted by wearing your game face all day, you can build a truer confidence by more intentionally focusing on cultivating many different parts of your voice so that no matter the leadership situation or audience you find yourself facing, you can respond in an authentic, constructive, and effective way. (Su, 2018, para. 1)

The voices that Su outlines are:

Character: This is your compass, the ideals that constitute your principles as a leader that anchor your leadership style. I discussed my principles in Chapter 1. If there is a better way to do it, we should do it that way... We should simplify our environment when we can . . . Trust people to do the job . . . Leaders don't create follow-ers; leaders create more leaders. This voice guides who you are as a leader and gives meaning to your actions and thoughts in your interactions with others.

Context: This is setting the stage for things that you need to commu-nicate to your team and to higher ups. This includes sharing with the people you lead to ensure that they have appropriate informa-tion to understand the reason behind decisions and the big pic-ture. This involves leading up as well as leading down. I include this in Chapter 3 when I discuss the Dean's Council. This group of advisers represented the different parts of the college, and helped me to provide context and information to faculty and staff.

Clarity: Your voice of clarity helps to ensure that we are focused on the most important priorities. I believe this is the art of knowing what to let go of and what to hold fast to. I asked my faculty and leadership team, "At the end of the year, how will we know that we have focused on the right things?" This was step one in having people think about the essential aspects of our jobs and to discard the rest. The clearest example of this idea during my first year was restructuring the way we implemented internships in the local schools. We made our systems leaner, more efficient, and more in line with best practices at other universities. As Su points out, your voice of clarity can include empowering your team to say no to things as well.

Curiosity: This voice involves asking questions, hearing people out, and making sure that all viewpoints are represented when at-tempting to solve a problem. This is not the same as having peo-ple give their viewpoints and then trying to make sure everyone is happy with a decision. It is making sure that all of the options are on the table for consideration. In my first year as dean, it seemed that I was constantly asking questions about why. Why do we do it that way? Part of asking this question was to see if there was, in fact, a better way to do things. It is also useful to hear people describe their understanding of a situation to see where they are coming from. We are all tied to our assumptions and shared understandings of the "way things are." Sometimes they are ac-curate, sometimes they aren't, but most people are acting on the best information that they have (usually handed down from those who came before). Well-intentioned, hard-working people can be stymied by systems that they haven't given much thought to changing. Let your voice of curiosity open the door to change.

Connection: This type of voice involves making connections with the people in your organization. Admittedly, during my first year, I was able to make connections with the leadership team more than the faculty as a whole. This wasn't intentional, but probably due to the fact that I worked most closely with this team to learn about the college and to focus on important initiatives in the college. Su (2018) recommends thanking and acknowledging your colleagues as an important step towards ensuring that you make connections with your colleagues. Engaging in storytelling and making time for rapport building at the start of meetings are two other ways to ensure these connections with your faculty.

The ideas that I have sketched out—framing, adaptive leadership, and voice—are three ideas that have helped me immensely during my first year. They are all ideas that I either discovered through reading or through experiences at conferences/institutes. These ideas have helped inform my decision-making during my first year of being a dean. These ideas are important because they point to the necessity of learning, multiple layers of understanding, and viewing leadership as a complex activity. The toolbox metaphor is (again) fitting. I view these three concepts as some of the most useful tools in my leadership repertoire.

Discovering these tools and learning about the efforts of other leaders helps me to do something else as well. It humbles me. I have come to the conclusion that good leaders humble themselves and recognize that leadership is more than technical fixes to technical problems. It ebbs and flows, waxes and wanes, shifts and evolves. Recognizing this fact is a necessary requirement to leading others.

Read, Read, Read

> *. . . having no opportunity to improve from example, let us read.*
> —George Washington

As I mentioned before, one piece of advice that I received prior to becoming a dean was to read. There are several layers of not-knowing that all new leaders possess. First of all, if you are an external hire, you do not know the context and environment of the place where you will lead. Simply put, from a cultural and social perspective, you don't know what you don't know. Second, you don't know what ideas about leadership will work in your new setting. The only way to know your context and environment is to experience it. Try, fail/succeed, learn, and try again. As Daniel Coyle writes in *The Talent Code* (2009), "Pick a target, reach for it, evaluate the gap between the target and the reach, and return to step one" (p. 92). The only way to learn about leadership ideas and styles is to study. I have spoken to other leaders in higher education about this idea, and some think of study/reading as extra work or something that one does in leisure time. I see it as a foundational part of the job of being a leader. It's not extra or something that you do when you have down time. It's integral to the way that I think of myself as a leader. The rationale is simple. There is simply no way that we could be exposed to the many great ideas about leadership without reading. In my work as a department chair and associate director, I set aside time in my daily routine (Chapter 7) to read about the craft and vocation of leadership. There is plenty of wisdom out there about how to lead, but we have to read in order to get it. I view reading about leadership in the same way I view writing/scholarship as a professor. It is a part of my job, I assign part of my day to this task, and I make sure that I write every day. The same can be said for learning to be a leader.

Engaging in self-study allows me to do something else. It allows me to enter into conversations with people who I'll never meet, but whose ideas I need to know about. It allows me to see problems, issues, and personalities through the perspective of other leaders. This is perhaps the most important part of self-study—the opportunity to learn from others who are engaging in the difficult task of leadership. It allows for a near constant self-reflection on the ways that I view myself as a leader, my successes and failures, and areas where I need to grow. Without reading and studying the thoughts of other leaders, I am not sure how this would take place. My guess is that I would still reflect on my strengths and shortcomings and that I would grow in my role as a leader, but it would just take much, much longer. I prefer to learn from others than to teach myself. In James Stavridis and R. Ancell's book *The Leader's Bookshelf* (2017), he lists reasons why leaders tend to be readers, and why reading helps us with our leadership development.

- Reading helps you to experiences events and ideas vicariously.
- Reading helps leaders to self-evaluate.
- Reading helps us to think about our heroes.
- Reading helps us to improve our communication skills.
- Reading helps us to improve our leadership skills. (pp. 2–5)

Through my studies and first year as a dean, I have come to realize that college leadership is a mix of art and science, but mostly art. There is an aspect of "not quite knowing if you are doing it right" that permeates my daily existence. I found myself in a continuous "acting-checking-evaluating" loop. It is comforting to know that other leaders, in other contexts, have experienced this same state of being. At the end of this chapter I have included a list of books that I read in the two years leading up to my first semester as dean. I include this list to emphasize that there are plenty of resources to assist and aid you in your transition from faculty to administration. The list includes resources on leadership at the chair, dean, and provost levels. It also includes books that focus on the practical and philosophical aspects of leading in higher education.

Experiences

In addition to internal leadership development workshops and programs at universities, most colleges and universities have funds set aside for the professional development of faculty and staff. When I was in Ohio, the institution I served had a great offering of professional development opportunities for faculty desiring to learn about leadership. I attended several workshops during my time there, including one titled "Implementing Title IX" and another titled "What Academic Administrators Need to Know." Several years ago, I began to actively seek out conferences, institutes, and programs that were specifically oriented towards leadership in higher education. As a faculty member I would attend my specific professional conference, and I would also look for opportunities to attend conferences oriented around college and university leadership at chair and dean levels. Above the funds reserved for faculty travel to conferences, many universities have additional monies for set aside for professional development, usually in the form of an internal competitive grants. I was able to secure funds like these in order to attend these events. One of the biggest take-aways for me is that if you are willing to look for money and seek out these learning experiences, they are not hard to find and attend. Another fact that I learned along the way is that many current deans are supportive of faculty who seek out these opportunities. In my experiences, deans and directors support this sort of activity because it, in the end, supports the overall functioning of the unit. The deans and directors that I worked with prior to my current position as a dean, were always supportive of my efforts to learn how to be a better leader. When speaking to your dean about your professional development and career ambitions, make your intentions explicit. Deans are always looking for energetic, talented people to join the ranks of administration.

Below I have included the official description of the conferences, institutes, and programs that I attended (or supported my faculty to attend) in the past 2 years. Again, these are just a few of the possible options for people who are interested in higher education leadership. This list is illustrative of the types of external experiences that are available for leaders who seek opportunities to learn and grow. During my first year as dean, I was always on the outlook for opportunities for my leadership team.

Harvard University, Management Development Program (MDP)

This intensive, two-week training program prepares mid-level managers early in their administrative experience with the skills to succeed in complex roles. Through real-world case studies, small group discussions, and interactive presentations, you will learn to think beyond your own administrative area and lead in ways that support larger institutional objectives. You will gain a deeper understanding of how different units function and will leave ready to incorporate broader strategic considerations into your management decisions. A hallmark of the HIHE experience is the formation of deep and lasting relationships among a diverse and dynamic cohort. Through MDP, you will have the opportunity to learn and network with colleagues across the cohort, as well as to make deeper connections among assigned small groups that meet throughout the duration of the two-week program and maintain connections well beyond. (https://www.gse.harvard.edu/ppe/program/management-development-program-mdp)

American Council on Education (ACE), Leadership Academy for Department Chairs

The ACE Leadership Academy for Department Chairs is a 2-day workshop that prepares department chairs for their roles as institutional leaders who can advance their programs and contribute to the larger mission of their colleges or universities. Under the guidance of experienced college and university leaders, participants explore best practices for leading departments in times of change. The format includes case studies, tabletop discussions, simulations on key leadership issues, and peer-to-peer sharing about achieving departmental success. (http://www.acenet.edu/leadership/programs/Pages/Leadership-Academy-for-Dept-Chairs.aspx)

Academic Chairpersons Conference

The Academic Chairpersons Conference is an annual forum where academic chairpersons, administrators and faculty from all areas of higher education share the most successful, innovative ideas and strategies to assist each other in becoming more effective in their positions. The conference format includes concurrent sessions of interactive workshops, best practice presentations and roundtable discussions. The emphasis of every conference is to provide practical, usable information in a climate of open discussion and collaborative exchange. Educational opportunities focus on departmental leadership including dealing with faculty and other personnel, determining effective budgets, handling student issues and developing pertinent curriculum. Conflict management, legal issues, fundraising, grant writing, finances and trends in higher education are conference topics of importance. New and seasoned department chairs receive tools that help them to deal with current situations and prepare for the future. (http://conferences.k-state .edu/academicchairpersons/about/general-information/)

▬▬▬▬

Penn State Academic Leadership Academy

The Academic Leadership Academy provides practical administrative knowledge and skills to academic administrators, including department heads, program directors, academic deans, vice presidents, and provosts. Many of these administrators are faced with difficult internal and external challenges. These challenges can prevent administrators from performing their duties effectively. Thus, appropriate professional development is helpful in fostering the necessary leadership skills. The curriculum will cover a range of important and practical subjects. The academy consists of both a summer on-site session and six virtual sessions throughout the following academic year. The on-site topics include Leadership Development, Organizational Dynamics, Shared Governance, Communication, Faculty Employment Issues, Faculty Development, Strategic Management, Budgeting, Conflict Resolution, and Organizational Change. (https://ed.psu.edu/ eps/academic-leadership-academy)

Books I Read Before Becoming Dean

Behling, L. (2014). *The resource handbook for academic deans.* San Francisco, CA: Jossey-Bass.

Berg, M., & Seeber, B. (2016). *The slow professor: Challenging the culture of speed in the academy.* Toronto, Canada: University of Toronto Press.

Bergquist, W., & Pawlak, K. (2008). *Engaging the six cultures of the academy.* San Francisco, CA: Jossey-Bass.

Bolman, L., & Deal, T. (2011). *Leading with soul: An uncommon journey of spirit.* San Francisco, CA: Jossey-Bass.

Bolman, L., & Deal, T. (2013). *Reframing organizations: Artistry, choice, and leadership.* San Francisco, CA: Jossey-Bass.

Bolman, L., & Gallos, J. (2011). *Reframing academic leadership.* San Francisco, CA: Jossey-Bass.

Bryant, P. (2005). *Confessions of an habitual administrator: An academic survival manual.* Bolton, MA: Anker.

Buller, J. (2007). *The essential academic dean: A practical guide to college leadership.* San Francisco, CA: Jossey-Bass.

Buller, J. (2010). *The essential college professor: A practical guide to an academic career.* San Francisco, CA: Jossey-Bass.

Buller, J. (2012). *The essential department chair: A comprehensive desk reference.* San Francisco, CA: Jossey-Bass.

Buller, J. (2013). *Positive academic leadership: How to stop putting out fires and start making a difference.* San Francisco, CA: Jossey-Bass.

Buller, J. (2015). Change leadership in higher education: A practical guide to academic transformation. San Francisco, CA: Jossey-Bass.

Burns, J. M. (2010). *Leadership.* New York, NY: Harper Perennial.

Chan, J.F. (2003). *Academic administrator's guide to meetings.* San Francisco, CA: Jossey-Bass.

Cipriano, R. (2011). *Facilitating a collegial department in higher education.* San Francisco, CA: Jossey-Bass.

Chu, D. (2012). The department chair primer: What chairs need to know and do to make a difference. San Francisco, CA: Jossey-Bass.

Collins, J. (2001). *Good to great: Why some companies make the leap ... and others don't.* New York, NY: Harper Business.

Coyle, D. (2009). *The talent code: Greatness isn't born. It's grown. Here's how.* New York, NY: Bantam Books.

Dalio, R. (2017). *Principles.* New York, NY: Simon & Schuster.

Davis, T. (2017). *Get better: 15 proven practices to build effective relationships at work.* New York, NY: Simon & Schuster.

Dethmer, J., Chapman, D., & Klemp, K. (2014). *The 15 commitments of conscious leadership: A new paradigm for sustainable success.* Denver, CO: KWK Press.

Duckworth, A. (2016). *Grit: The power of passion and perseverance.* New York, NY: Scribner.

Ferriss, T. (2017). *Tribe of mentors: Short life advice from the best in the world.* Boston, MA: Houghton Mifflin Harcourt.

Friedman, R. (2014). *The best place to work: The art and science of creating an extraordinary workplace.* New York, NY: Perigee Books.

Fullan, M., & Scott, G. (2009). *Turnaround leadership for higher education.* San Francisco, CA: Jossey-Bass.

Goleman, D. (2013). *Focus: The hidden driver of excellence.* New York, NY: HarperCollins.

Goleman, D. (2017). *What makes a leader?* Boston, MA: Harvard Business Review Press.

Gmelch, W., & Buller, J. (2015). *Building academic leadership capacity: A guide to best practices.* San Francisco, CA: Jossey-Bass.

Gmelch, W., Hopkins, D., & Damico, S. (2011). *Seasons of a dean's life: Understanding the role and building leadership capacity.* Sterling, VA: Stylus.

Gmelch, W., & Wolverton, M. (2002). *College deans: Leading from within.* Westport, CT: Greenwood.

Goldsmith, M. (2007). *What got you here won't get you there: How successful people become even more successful.* New York, NY: Hyperion.

Hadeed, K. (2017). *Permission to screw up: How I learned to lead by doing (almost) everything wrong.* New York, NY: Penguin Press.

Heifetz, R. (1994). *Leadership without easy answers.* Cambridge, MA: Harvard University Press.

Heifetz, R., Grashow, A., & Linsky, M. (2009). *The practice of adaptive leadership: Tools and tactics for changing your organization and the world.* Boston, MA: Harvard Business Review Press.

Hendrickson, R., Lane, J., Harris, J., & Dorman, R. (2013). *Academic leadership and governance of higher education: A guide for trustees, leaders, and aspiring leaders of two- and four-year institutions.* Sterling, VA: Stylus.

Holiday, R., & Hanselman, S. (2016). *The daily stoic: 366 meditations on wisdom, perseverance, and the art of living.* New York, NY: Penguin Press.

Kabat-Zinn, J. (2005). *Wherever you go, there you are: Mindfulness meditation in everyday life.* New York, NY: Hyperion.

Kabat-Zinn, J. (2006). *Coming to our senses: Healing ourselves and the world through mindfulness.* New York, NY: Hatchette Books.

Kouzes, J. M., & Posner, B. Z. (2003). *Academic administrators guide to exemplary leadership.* San Francisco, CA: Jossey-Bass.

Leaming, D. R. (2007). *Academic leadership: A practical guide to chairing the department.* Bolton, MA: Anker.

Lees, N. D. (2006). *Chairing academic departments: Traditional and emerging expectations.* Bolton, MA: Anker.

Lucas, A., & Associates. (2000). *Leading academic change. Essential roles for department chairs.* San Francisco, CA: Jossey-Bass.

Marquet, L. D. (2012). *Turn the ship around! A true story of turning followers into leaders.* New York, NY: Penguin Press.

Newport, C. (2016). *Deep work: Rules for focused success in a distracted world.* New York, NY: Hatchette Books.

Nielsen, L. (2013). *Provost: Experiences, reflections and advice from a former "number two" on campus.* New York, NY: Stylus.

Rose, T. (2015). *The end of average: How we succeed in a world that values sameness.* New York, NY: Harper.

Sample, S. (2002. *The contrarian's guide to leadership.* San Francisco, CA: Jossey-Bass.

Seldin, P. (2004). *The teaching portfolio: A practical guide to improved performance and promotion/tenure decisions.* Bolton, MA: Anker.

Schulz, K. (2010). *Being wrong: Adventures in the margin of error.* New York, NY: Harper.

Silva, P. J. (2007). *How to write a lot: A practical guide to productive academic writing.* Washington, DC: APA.

Sinek, S. (2009). *Start with why: How great leaders inspire everyone to take action.* New York, NY: Penguin Press.

Sinek, S. (2017). *Leaders eat last: Why some teams pull together and others don't.* New York, NY: Penguin Press.

Smith, R. V. (2006). *Where you stand is where you sit: An academic administrator's handbook.* Fayetteville: University of Arkansas Press.

Stark, P., & Flaherty, J. (2010). *The only leadership book you'll ever need: How to build organizations where employees love to come to work.* Franklin Lakes, NJ: Career Press.

Stavridis, J., & Ancell, R. M. (2017). *The leader's bookshelf.* Annapolis, MD: Naval Institute Press.

Sutton, R. (2007). *The no asshole rule: Building a civilized workplace and surviving one that isn't.* New York, NY: Business Plus.

Ward, L., Siegel, M., & Davenport, Z. (2012). *First-generation college students: Understanding and improving the experience from recruitment to commencement.* San Francisco, CA: Jossey-Bass.

Wheeler, D. W., Seagren, A. T., Becker, L. W., Kinley, E. R., Mlinek, D. D., & Robson, K. J. (2008). *The academic chair's handbook.* San Francisco, CA: Jossey-Bass.

Wheeler, D.W. (2012). *Servant leadership for higher education: Principles and practices.* San Francisco, CA: Jossey-Bass.

Willink, J., & Babin, L. (2015). *Extreme ownership: How U.S. Navy seals lead and win.* New York, NY: St. Martin's Press.

Wooden, J. (1997). *Wooden: A lifetime of observations and reflections on and off the court.* New York, NY: McGraw-Hill.

References

Bolman, L., & Deal, T. (2013). *Reframing organizations: Artistry, choice, and leadership.* San Francisco, CA: Jossey-Bass.

Bolman, L., & Gallos, J. (2011). *Reframing academic leadership.* San Francisco, CA: Jossey-Bass.

Coyle, D. (2009). *The talent code: Greatness isn't born. It's grown. Here's how.* New York, NY: Bantam Books.

Heifetz, R. (1994). *Leadership without easy answers.* Cambridge, MA: Harvard University Press.

Heifetz, R., Grashow, A., & Linsky, M. (2009). *The practice of adaptive leadership: Tools and tactics for changing your organization and the world.* Cambridge, MA: Harvard University Press.

Maslow, A. (1969). *The psychology of science: A reconnaissance.* Nevada City, CA: Gateway Books.

Stavridis, J., & Ancell, R.M. (2017). *The leader's bookshelf.* Annapolis, MD: Naval Institute Press.

Su, J.A. (2018). You don't just need one leadership voice—you need many. *Harvard Business Review,* (January 10), Retrieved from https://hbr .org/2018/01/you-dont-just-need-one-leadership-voice-you-need-many

3

Ask for Help (You're Going to Need It)

People are not your most important asset. The right people are.
—Jim Collins

BIG IDEA FOR THIS CHAPTER

In my first year, one of the most important things I did was to ask for help. When you are an external hire to be a dean, there is no way that you can know all that you need to know, so you are dependent on the knowledge and leadership of others. This fact forces you to learn from faculty, chairs, staff members, and other deans. Ambiguity and ignorance are an integral part of the first-year experience. To help navigate this environment, I created a Dean's Council to help me lead the college. Creating this group and leaning on their knowledge and wisdom was the best decision I made during my first year. I conclude this chapter by sharing what we did and talked about at our monthly meetings.

One of the best books that I read during the months leading up to taking my first dean's position was Jim Collin's *Good to Great: Why Some Companies Make the Leap . . . and Others Don't* (2001). In this book, Collins and his team examined the factors that separate great companies from those that are simply good. He looked at ideas like "Level 5" leadership, discipline, simplifying goals, and technology. Although this is a book about business, Collins writes, "I see my work as being about discovering what creates enduring great enterprises of any type" (p. 15). I connect much of what Collins has to say about successful organizations to his idea that the right people are what matters most. The line from his book—"Get the right people on the bus"—resonated with me during my first year experiences. I spent the first month of my time as dean deciding on who would be on my leadership team, the Dean's Council. When deciding my leadership team, I kept Collins' advice at the forefront of my decision-making: First who, then what. First, focus on who is on the team; second, focus on strategy, decisions, and the real work. "Good-to-great management teams consist of people who debate vigorously in search of the best answers, yet who unify behind decisions, regardless of parochial interests" (p. 63).

Knowing That You Don't Know: Finding Your 3rd Base Coach

I started teaching middle school social studies (world history, geography, civics) when I was 21 years old. As is customary in a lot of small rural schools, I was also the varsity baseball coach and middle school football coach. This part of the job and my role in filling it was a very brief part of my formal interview for the teaching position that I got. After a good interview with the school principal, I was offered the teaching portion of the job. I am sure it was written on my face that I was very excited to be offered a teaching job so early in my search. After accepting the job and thanking the principal for his time, he said that there was "one more thing" that he wanted to discuss.

"You know. We have an opening for our varsity baseball coaching position, and we need someone to fill it for this upcoming spring." Note that this interview was in December, and baseball started in late February. Having no desire to coach baseball, I politely declined his offer. He pressed on.

"Well, we really need a baseball coach, and I think you'd be great for the job."

Sensing his change in voice and stressing of the word "really" it became clear that this interview was for two jobs: teacher and coach. I tried to make my case.

"I am flattered by the offer, but I know how hard teaching can be. I just finished my student teaching, and it was the hardest work I have ever done. I'd really like to focus on being the best teacher I can be, get my feet wet, and maybe try coaching in a couple years."

The principal just repeated himself. "Well, we really need a baseball coach, and I think you'd be great for the job."

I relented and accepted both jobs. Honestly, I wanted to teach so badly, that I would have taken on any additional responsibilities that he gave me—which he did. Part of the reason for not wanting to coach was that I wanted to be a good teacher and I didn't want to be overburdened. That was an honest assessment, and that's what I told him during the interview. I didn't even like the sport of baseball. I had played as a kid in school, but mostly because it was something to do with my friends. I even skipped my senior season because I found it boring. The reason that this job scared me the most was the uncertainty of being the new guy. The new guy in charge of a group of 15–19-year-olds. I would be leading a group of guys who were pretty close to the same age as me. I didn't feel that I had the experience or the knowledge to coach. The whole idea of coaching a sport I didn't know that much about seemed crazy.

Since this job started in January, I got about six weeks of teaching under my belt before I began to think seriously about being the varsity baseball coach. We had tryouts in mid-February, and our first players' meeting after school in early March. I can still remember how anxious I was to meet with the team for the first time. At the meeting I went over team rules, practice and game schedule, and set general expectations for the season. I told them a little about myself and my background. Overall, the meeting was really pretty standard, and I thought it went well. As the meeting started and the players began to file in, I noticed that some of the players' parents also attended, which was fine. I had told the guys that we were meeting after school for this first meeting and that their parents could attend. I noticed two guys, presumably fathers of players, who came to the meeting who stood in the back of the room. They were dressed normally and they were wearing shirts, jackets, and hats that had the school's logo on them. As the meeting unfolded there were two thoughts running through my head: the meeting agenda and these two guys. I had played sports throughout my childhood, and I knew that these two dads were probably the guys that had coached these boys since they were five years old. That's usually the way baseball worked in this area. Boys started playing baseball around 5–6, and a couple dads served and volunteered their time to coach the group. Many times, the same group of parents would coach the boys in little league up until their time in high school.

In that meeting, I made a decision to speak to these guys afterward to see what their experiences were with this group of boys, and I was right. They were the "team dads" that had coached these boys since they were all in t-ball. After most of the players had left the meeting, I sat down with these two guys and basically hired them to help me coach (although the job was volunteer, no money in the budget to pay assistant coaches). My rationale was simple. These two fathers knew the strengths and weaknesses of the players. They had coached baseball for over a decade. And, I could learn from them. I knew what I didn't know, and they could provide that experience and knowledge. As the first couple of weeks unfolded, it was clear that I had made the right decision. They helped me with practices, strategy, and well, anything else I asked them to help me with. They were eager to help because they loved this group of guys and wanted to see them succeed. When the first game approached, one of the dads, Keith, was talking to me about filling out the line-up card to give the umpire at home plate before the game started. Of course, I had never done this, and he helped. When the game was about to begin, he gave me some words of encouragement, and began to walk towards first base. I was standing in front of the dugout near third base.

In high school baseball it is customary for the head coach to stand at third base to manage the game. This person gives batters appropriate signals and serves to make the decision of whether or not to send players home or not. The coach that stands on first base has an easier job. You encourage batters, talk to players who get on base, and direct players to go to second base, if, your judgment, you think they can make it without getting thrown out. In the pecking order of authority and judgment, the coach at third base is more important. The third base coach manages the game. Out of respect for my position as the "head coach," Keith assumed that I would be manning the post at third base. Out of my recognition for his experience and love for baseball and these boys, I disagreed. He was the right person to coach the team from third base. I called his name and said, "I think you should coach third base. It makes more sense. I can take first."

"But you're the head coach."

"That doesn't matter. We want to win don't we? Of course we do. We need you at third."

Keith didn't hesitate. He walked over to third base and began to coach those boys as he had done since they were in t-ball. Later in the game, he mentioned to me that I could take over third base in a couple games. I nodded at the suggestion, but I never did take over third base. Keith was the right person for that job. As the head coach, my job was to put the team in the best position to win.

This was a lesson that was key to any of the other leadership positions that I took in future jobs and one that I recommend to new deans. When you become a dean, no matter if you are an internal candidate or someone from the outside, there are always going to be people in your college who know more than you do about something. There are always Keiths in your college that you should tap to be your third base coach. Depending on their experiences with your predecessors, they may not be used to being utilized as I am describing, but the sooner you decide you need help in an area (i.e., assessment, scheduling, community relations) and the sooner you bring knowledgeable people into your team, the better. This is what good leaders do. We leave our egos out of the equation and seek help. We realize that the team's success is more important than any one thing that we could do by ourselves. It also forms a bond between the leader and the team that sends the message that everyone has role to play and something to contribute.

Colleges in the 21st century, especially colleges of education, are simply too complex for one person to make all of the necessary decisions—accreditation, assessment, faculty evaluation, field work, internships, fundraising, community and school partnerships, scholarships, student issues, new programs, state regulations, committee work, etc. It's simply not possible to know everything about the different aspects of the college, maintain relationships with faculty, work with upper administration, and be equipped to make high-level decisions. I have often reflected on job advertisements for deans and provost positions in higher education. Scanning the advertisements in *The Chronicle of Higher Education* or *higheredjobs.com* one is left with the feeling that the person being described in the ad isn't a person after all, but a super human being (and this doesn't even include the responsibilities that aren't listed). The level and volume of tasks that deans are responsible for maintaining sounds impossible. The truth is that it is impossible, if you tried to do it all by yourself. In fact, that was one of ideas that freaked me out about applying for a dean's position. How is one person supposed to do all of the things that are being described in the "responsibilities" section of this job announcement? The answer is simple. Good deans find a third base coach. Find yours.

Building Leadership Capacity

I start with the premise that the function of leadership is to produce more leaders, not more followers.

—Ralph Nader

Figure 3.1 is one that I sketched out one morning when thinking about this chapter. It represents how I see leadership and its impact on the people we lead. Information and authority to make decisions should not reside solely with the leader, but should be distributed across the organization. This is the spirit behind the quote at the beginning of this section: the function of leadership is to produce more leaders, not more followers. At the most basic level, building leadership capacity is about developing leaders to be "change capable." In their book *Turnaround Leadership for Higher Education*, Fullan and Scott (2009) write that universities need to become more "change capable" to meet demands of the 21st century (pp. 76–78).

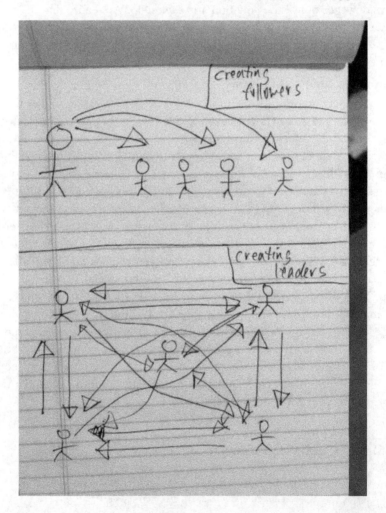

Figure 3.1

My efforts around building leadership capacity within the college were directed at my leadership team and constituted a more informal, monthly meeting. Other universities have more formalized leadership capacity building programs. For instance, Northern Kentucky University (NKU) has a program for leaders within their college of education that culminates with examining a "Problem of Practice" within the college that they attempt to solve. The experiences that I had with my leadership team were not this formal, but I was attempting to accomplish many of the same goals as the NKU program. In the future, I intend to have a more formal leadership capacity program. I attended a presentation at an education conference in the middle of my first semester in which I learned about NKU's program. Their program has four underlying assumptions that were more explicit than my attempts that first semester. Their program assumes that:

- The higher education context is changing exponentially—and leadership networks that are "change-capable" are essential.
- We operate within an ecosystem—context matters.
- Where we focus our attention and energies matters.
- Leadership can be developed and nurtured (Crites, Reed, & Runge, 2017).

Permission to be Great

One of the first meetings that I had as a new dean was with one of my department chairs. We discussed a new and innovative program that she and her department were considering. The idea involved a new TESOL (Teaching English to Speakers of Other Languages) program and recruiting international students to the program. Some of our faculty had connections to China and Japan, and it sounded like a great opportunity. The excitement about her idea and the possibilities of having this program were obvious. Equally as obvious was her nervousness about pitching her idea to the new dean. On several occasions, she commented, "Now. Before you say 'no,' let me explain why this will work." It seemed like a strange way to frame a project that you already thought was great. Once she finished explaining the new program, the pros and cons, and the students it would serve, she asked, "So. What do you think? Can we do this?"

The question she asked, on its face, is a very basic question. It was her tone of voice and facial expression that didn't fit. It didn't fit the preceding conversation about her great idea. For 10–15 minutes she explained the ins and outs of a program in TESOL, why it was a good idea, why it could boost enrollment, and how it was an innovative program for a small college like ours. When she talked about her idea, she was proud. She was proud of what might be and the potential impact that it could have for students around the world (literally). But, when she finished her pitch, her demeanor changed to one of doubt and skepticism. The change, on the surface, was quite pronounced, when she asked what I thought of her idea. Sensing her anxiety, I simply repeated her question back to her.

"Well. What do you think? Do you think we can do this? Why shouldn't we have this program?"

She launched into repeating herself from her previous comments, and I stopped her.

"Do you think it's a good idea? Are there any drawbacks to going down this road that you haven't considered?"

She told me about the contacts that she had across the university and in East Asia. She told me how other universities implement this program. She talked about our resources and how we could make sure that these courses were created and staffed to make the program viable. I repeated my questions.

"What do you think? Do you think we can do this? Why shouldn't we have this program?"

In repeating my question, I was attempting to guide my department chair to the obvious answer. The obvious answer is yes. Yes. We should have this program. We should have this program because it's a good idea and you have done the necessary work to determine if it would flourish at our institution. She was waiting on me to determine or judge whether or not her idea was good enough, right after she spent ten minutes telling me that her idea was great.

To repeat, colleges and universities are simply too complex to run by yourself. This is about trusting other people to do the right things. We have to put our trust in our people if we expect them to place their trust in us. Expecting that people will rise to the occasion should be our default position, not the other way around. Positive expectations become self-fulfilling. We expect the best from people and they rise to the occasion. It works in the other direction as well. Low expectations for your people ensures that is what you will get. Most people know this intuitively, but in practice we see leaders trying to lead without empowering faculty or making any attempt to develop the next set of leaders. Ask yourself this question: If you were taken out of your college, what would happen to the operations of the organization? The first semester I served as dean, I routinely found myself asking the following questions. When you are in a new leadership role, they can help to clarify what's being done, by whom, and if things are working. These questions don't usually lead to the full picture, but they are a necessary first step.

- What's the process for this?
- Who is responsible for this?
- Why are we doing it this way?

Who's On Your Team?

Diversity in counsel, unity in command.
—Cyrus the Great (King of Persia)

The most important decision that I made during my first year was to create and utilize a core leadership team. I say "core" here because there were leaders in the college that were not a part of this formal group. In fact, there were leaders in every department and program. This group, however, was the "Dean's Council," and they helped me examine global issues in the college as well as served as an advisory board for me. Below I discuss some general tips for creating a leadership counsel for your college.

1. **Draw the boundaries:** The metaphor that I find helpful in beginning this process comes from cartography/geography. Imagine a blank map of a continent with no political boundaries separating the countries. Take the continent of South America for instance. Visualize the map of the entire landmass without boundaries showing where Brazil, Argentina, and Columbia are located relative to other countries. As the leader developing a leadership group where one doesn't exist, these boundaries have to be drawn. When assembling this group, think about the different parts of the college and/or the big jobs that need to be done. For my college, some of these parts were clearly defined and some were not. On the "clear" side of the ledger, I had my department chairs. Department chairs have typical and expected roles within their departments like scheduling, faculty evaluations, dealing with student complaints, etc. On the other side, the boundaries were less clear. The big tasks were obvious, but the boundaries were not. Therein lies the problem: we had some important things to get done, but no clear boundaries defining where these jobs belonged and who was responsible for them. I know that my college was engaged in accreditation, assessment, teacher licensure, and partnerships with local schools. It was

less clear who those jobs belonged to. Make this clearer by drawing boundaries.

2. **Look around/observe:** This is related to number one. Before you can assemble your team, you need to look around and see how things actually operate in the college. Many times, there will be official statements or documents about how things are supposed to be done (sometimes these are absent). Some of this will be found in faculty handbooks, job descriptions, or HR documents. But that doesn't mean that tasks and jobs are actually conducted according to these statements. Looking around for several weeks allows us to see if these documents and people's actions are aligned. If you do not have a leadership team in place, you will need to take some time to determine what roles will be (#1), and then choose the right people to fill these roles. Since the department chairs were already in place and since they represented a level of leadership that I wanted on the team, I leaned on them for advice on what and who we needed on the team.

3. **Create titles and roles to fit your needs:** Although there were leaders in the college, their roles were largely implicit and informal. If we are interested in helping create leaders within our organizations, we need to be clear about what we are asking people to do. Part of this clarity comes from what people are actually called. A case in point is the associate dean, who was already in place when I arrived. He, like most associate deans, had a job description that mostly determined what he did in that role. This is to say that there was partial alignment between his job description and what he did on a day-to-day basis. He didn't feel that people in the college actually knew what his role was, which was assessment and accreditation. With this in mind, we decided to change his title from "associate dean" to "associate dean of accreditation and assessment." This small change in his title helped him because when he is working with faculty on these matters, it helps them to frame him as a leader in these areas. This is a very simple solution to the issue of clarity around roles.

4. **Staff leaders:** I spent my first month on the job trying to learn as much as I could about how things in the college operated. While I was doing this, I was looking for a handful of people to be on the leadership team. I intentionally decided to have a staff member (i.e., non-faculty) on my team. This was a culture shift for this particular college for two reasons. First, they didn't have a leadership team in place before I arrived. Formal leadership was primarily thought of as residing with the dean and department chairs. Secondly, staff was viewed as being primarily a support role, which is quite common

for organizations. I wanted to reverse this trend. In my first weeks on the job, it was clear that the staff who had worked in this college knew more about operations and functions that the faculty did. Perhaps this is the way it should be. Faculty are consumed with teaching, working with students, scholarship, and general service to the university. Faculty attend to the academic mission of the college, and staff attend to making sure that key operations to run the college actually work and are efficient. The staff member that I chose to be on the leadership team had been at the university for over 30 years, had worked in several key offices on campus (i.e., registrar), and was now the key contact person for the State Department of Education for our licensing needs. She possessed an expertise and institutional knowledge that was different from anyone else in the college. She was the longest serving staff member in the college, so she brought a unique point of view to the issues we discussed in the Dean's Council. Near the end of the first semester, I also added my administrative assistant (i.e., academic associate to the dean) to the team as well. Her knowledge of the university and talents at helping to run the college were invaluable to me during my first year. She was a great addition to an already strong team of leaders. As a new leader, you need smart, knowledgeable people at the table. Staff included.

5. **Revisiting the boundaries you drew (#1):** At some point in the first year, it's a good idea to revisit the boundaries that you drew at the beginning of this process. Oftentimes there are tasks that were carried out by someone that now resides in another subunit. These conversations need to happen sooner rather than later to ensure that new protocols and mindsets are developed. Prior to my arrival, the field office and the chairs managed internships. This created confusion because there wasn't a clear idea of who made the final decisions about intern placements. We decided to let the Director of Teacher Education be the final authority on these matters. This created clarity for faculty and students alike. Creating a leadership team where one didn't exist, adding to an existing group, or revising established roles is key to ensuring that your leaders are in fact, leading the organization. The first year I was in the dean's role, the team discussed this at the end of the fall semester and at the end of the spring semester. At our meetings, we focused and discussed the following questions:

    – Is your role as a leader in this college explicit enough? What can we be clearer about?
    – Is there alignment between your stated roles and what you actually do?
    – What's working? Not working?

6. **Regular meetings:** During my first year, the Dean's Council met the third Friday of each month. These regularly scheduled meetings were used to talking about college issues, common problems that we could collectively solve, and develop our leadership capacity. These meetings also helped us to establish expectations and to support each other. One of the basic premises of our meetings, relative to leadership capacity and development, was to provide ongoing support and conversation about what it means to lead in the organization. This is about developing our current leaders, but it is also about setting the stage for leadership succession. Who will lead the college after us? Will there be a culture of collaboration and cooperation in place for the next group of leaders in the college? This council ensures that we will hand over a better college to future leaders than what we inherited. I believe this is a responsibility of the group. Make improvements in all areas of what we do, and when it's time to turn over the reins to the next leaders, we are handing over a college where the culture is conducive to doing good work. In those areas where we weren't successful in making things better, the next set of leaders can take up those causes.

7. **The good, the bad, and the ugly:** I made it clear that I wanted our Council and our meetings to be a place where the leaders in the college could share the good parts of our jobs (the successes), the bad parts (the tough days), and the ugly parts (our failures). Most people in leadership are pretty good at the first two: we like to talk about our successes and we like to complain about things that aren't working as well as we'd like. Talking about failure is something that we aren't good at because it's painful. It reveals in us a weakness that we feel damages our credibility and reputation with the group. In an attempt to fix this desire to ignore our failures, I made a conscious effort to highlight my failures to the leadership team. I believe that trying something and failing is a part of personal growth and learning to be a leader. I will talk more about this in Chapter 8.

What We Did My First Semester

"We operate within an ecosystem—context matters,"—this was one of the most important realizations of my efforts to build leadership capacity my first year. The context of our college included a new dean, a change in responsibility for the newly formed leadership team, a less than ideal relationship with the local schools, and attempts to develop the university's first doctoral program. Part of my thinking in developing a leadership team was rooted in the scholarship around leadership capacity. This includes adhering to proven leadership (vs. management) models, strategic thinking, faculty coaching, managing conflict, and leading change (Gmelch & Buller, 2015). But, for me, my intention was to learn about leading this college along with the newly formed leadership team.

For leaders who are developing a leadership team or dean's council for the purpose of developing leadership capacity, below is a month-by-month sketch of what we did in our meetings the first semester. This list is not intended to be a model or template for others to follow because each college will have specific areas that they need to focus on to make the college operations better. As I said before, the purpose of forming a dean's council was to:

1. serve as an advisory group
2. examine issues in the college from a global perspective
3. make decisions that served to help the group
4. build leadership capacity where none existed before.

Although these purposes were not rank ordered, I soon came to realize that the more we did #4 (building leadership capacity), the better we were able to do #2 and #3 (examine issues and make decisions). The other thing to consider/reflect on when creating a leadership team where one did not exist before—it takes time and patience. People come to this team with different experiences, frames of reference, and expectations. Coming together to look at these issues allows your team to check their reality against the reality of others. It serves as a check on our subjective biases and allows us to see college issues through other people's perspectives.

September Meeting

At our first meeting, my goal was to frame our leadership team as a group that would serve as an advisory group, but also a group that I'd like to learn with. Although our group was not as focused on developing leadership capacity as the example that I used before (NKU), thinking about leadership was definitely a goal that I had in mind for our meetings. For this first meeting I had several handouts for the group. These included the "4 frames cheat sheet," a bibliography of leadership books (see Chapter 2), and a copy of the book *Reframing Academic Leadership* (Bolman & Gallos, 2011). I introduced the group to the idea of framing and talked about how I approached problems. Over the course of the conversation with the team they discussed of problems within the college and what frame(s) could be applied. Ahead of the meeting, I also sent the group a video from YouTube titled, "Why Good

Leaders Make You Feel Safe" by Simon Sinek (Sinek, 2014). (TED Talk description: What makes a great leader? Management theorist Simon Sinek suggests, it's someone who makes their employees feel secure, who draws staffers into a circle of trust. But creating trust and safety—especially in an uneven economy—means taking on big responsibility.)

I closed the meeting by talking about the following points.

1. Making decisions within your area of influence.
   – This is the hallmark of being a professional.
2. Leaders don't create followers. Leaders create more leaders.
   – Are you doing this in your areas of influence?
3. Don't condemn. Coach your team up.
   – No one is great at everything.
4. Instead of focusing on being right, focus on getting it right.
   – Allow other people to win.
5. Our success is tied to one another. If you don't succeed, we don't succeed.
   – What's your mindset?
6. Radical candor
   – Respectfully, say what needs to be said.

After the first meeting, I created a Google Doc for the leadership team to help me keep up with our many (future) accomplishments. Here is the actual email that I wrote to the team:

> I have started a googledoc where I'd like for us to keep a running list of our accomplishments and improvements as a College. When you or someone in your area does something awesome, let's add it to the list.

> Here's my thinking...I was thinking about our 'last' faculty meeting of this year. The one that will happen in April 2018. I would like for us to be able to look back on the year and celebrate how far we've come as a College. Victories small and victories large...let's add to the list. I have already started it...see link below. Being great is a process. Let's document the process...(personal communication, September 24, 2017)

October Meeting

Between our first and second meetings, we had an episode within the university that dealt with a personnel decision. This decision created a fair amount of gossip, some of which got back to members of the leadership team. Having seen the destructive force of gossip go unchecked and how damaging it can be, I decided to discuss the idea of gossip (and how to stop it) at our October meeting. Here is the actual email that I wrote to the team:

> I am sending some materials ahead of our Dean's Council meeting on Friday. There are a couple of concepts/ideas I'd like for us to think about. One is in the 'human resources and political' frames and the other is more inward facing, your leadership orientation.
>
> The first idea I'd like for us to think about is the culture around gossip.
>
> 1. What are the norms and accepted ways of viewing gossip?
> 2. Is it rewarded?
> 3. What impact does it have on the people we serve in our areas of influence?
> 4. Do we want a culture of loyalty or a culture of trust?
>
> I have included three quick reads on this as well.
>
> 1. https://www.tlnt.com/the-terribly-destructive-impact-of-workplace-gossip/
> 2. https://www.inc.com/marcel-schwantes/if-you-do-these-things-you-qualify-as-a-gossiper-which-research-says-can-ruin-yo.html
> 3. https://hbr.org/2015/01/stop-enabling-gossip-on-your-team
>
> The second idea is your leadership orientation, based on the Reframing Academic Leadership book that I gave you all at our first meeting. The six question survey/quiz is attached (http://www.leebolman.com/Leadership%20Orientations.pdf). Give this a look before the meeting. (personal communication, October 20, 2018)

The majority of this meeting revolved around discussing the questions above. Members of the leadership team shared their experiences with gossip within the college and how it had operated in the past. Gossip, as is the case in many organizations, served as a form of currency. It had value to the people participating and was damaging to the people that were the subject of the gossip. That day I asked the leadership team to help me create a different atmosphere around gossip. The idea was simple. Diminish the value that gossip has and it will no longer be useful for people to engage in the process. When people attempt to bring you in to gossip, refuse to participate. Repeat: refuse to participate and it dies. A member of the team asked a pointed question: "What should we tell people who do this?" I then shared a template that I used in my time as a department chair.

"When people within the college come to you with gossip, just refuse to involve yourself. Here is what I say. I am sure there are more elegant ways of saying this, but I have found that this works for me. I say,

1. This sounds like gossip.

2. I don't want to participate in this.
3. Do you have something important that you want to discuss?"

The rest of the meeting we looked at the results of our self-assessment from the quiz that I sent to the team. This simple quiz had six questions that highlighted their strengths and weaknesses of "leadership orientation." After the results were tabulated, the team was able to see where their leadership strengths were located among the four frames of structural, human resource, political, and symbolic. Although the team members were not surprised by their own scores, it was helpful to have people discuss their areas of strength with the group. A very interesting picture of the leadership team emerged—one team member's weaknesses represented another member's strengths. A passage from *Buller's Positive Academic Leadership* (2013) is appropriate here: "... make the best use of different individuals' strongest assets, creating work groups and task forces, taking full advantage of opportunities as they arise, and *using the gifts* of one person to compensate for the *challenges of another*" [emphasis added] (p. 12).

December Meeting

At our December meeting, we discussed the idea of emotional intelligence (EI), and how it could help the college leadership rethink how to lead our respective units. I gave each member of the Dean's Council a copy of Daniel Goleman's small volume *What Makes a Leader?* (Goleman, 2017). Goleman argues that EI is what separates good leaders from great leaders: "It isn't IQ or technical skills. It's emotional intelligence: A group of five skills that enable the best leaders to maximize their own and their followers' performance" (p. 59). We can learn these skills—self-awareness, self-regulation, motivation, empathy, social skill—through "persistence, practice, and feedback from colleagues" ... (p. 60). It is/was my goal to make my leadership team aware of how EI matters more than just about anything else when leading a team. It was my plan to coach up the team in these areas whenever possible, and not only make these ideas an explicit part of our formal meetings, but also in our daily interactions with each other.

We also discussed a short video from YouTube titled *Why Incompetent People Think They're Amazing: An Animated Lesson—David Dunning* (Dunning, 2017). (TED Ed description: It looks at how humans frequently overestimate our abilities in certain areas. In short, we aren't very good at evaluating ourselves accurately. This is called the Dunning-Kruger Effect. In fact, those with the lowest abilities in certain areas are the most likely to overrate themselves.) The video reminds us that "We all have pockets of incompetence that we don't recognize." The point of this concept for a leadership team is clear: we have to point out and recognize our weaknesses so we can improve. I also see this idea fitting nicely with the findings on EI. The video concludes by advising people to solicit feedback (and actually take it to heart) and to keep learning. Learning helps eliminate the weaknesses that we have.

If the first two items (emotional intelligence and Dunning-Kruger Effect) we discussed were theoretical and research based, the last item was practical in nature. I gave the Dean's Council a copy of C. K. Gunsalus' (2011) white paper "Basic Guidelines for Handling Complaints." This is a 40-page document that outlines ways to deal with the routine nature of handling complaints. My favorite part of the paper is the third section that outlines "Ten Guidelines" for doing this. This is the section that we briefly discussed in the meeting because I think it is the most applicable to the daily work of the leaders in the college. It's the most practical and user-friendly part of the document. I also suggested that the leadership team share these ideas with leaders in their areas of influence as well. If these ideas were great for the Dean's Council, they'd be good for other leaders in the college as well.

Leaders Not on the Dean's Council

The months leading up to taking the Dean position were very busy. I was wrapping up my responsibilities at my previous institution, getting my house ready to sell, finding a place to live, researching schools for my son, and a host of other tasks. During that time frame I also studied the backgrounds of the people in the college I would be leading. In that process I discovered something that helped me to think about how I would lead once I arrived. When I looked into the backgrounds of my faculty, one fact emerged. The faculty at this institution was full of people who had served in leadership roles during their careers. Specifically, there were former school leaders, former district leaders, people with experience leading departments, and professors who were teacher leaders. It became clear to me that in this job, I would be leading other leaders. This is the default position that I carried with me into the job and that sustained me throughout my first year.

During the first couple weeks I was on the job, I met with as many faculty as I could. I wanted to put names with faces and introduce myself. Since I had already done my homework on them before I arrived, I often asked about their previous work in education. And, I did something that I suggest that all new deans do. I reached out to the most senior leaders in the college and asked them if I could come to them for advice from time to time. In those meetings, I would say, "I know that you have been a school leader before. I am brand new in this role. I'd like to be able to come to you from time to time for advice. Can I do this?" Predictably, the leaders in my college were more than willing to help me become a better leader. Every time.

The reasoning is simple and straightforward. I was saying: You are experienced in this field. You have been a successful leader before. I want to learn from you. Will you teach me what you know?

Work on thinking about your leadership position in this way. I want to learn from you. Will you teach me what you know?

On my most difficult days as a rookie dean, these wise people gave me counsel that proved to be invaluable. Be careful to not overlook the wisdom of people who work in the same hall as you. They are there. They are always there. Ask for help.

References

Bolman, L., & Gallos, J. (2011). *Reframing academic leadership.* San Francisco, CA: Jossey-Bass.

Buller, J. (2013). *Positive academic leadership: How to stop putting out fires and start making a difference.* San Francisco, CA: Jossey-Bass.

Collins, J. (2001). *Good to great: Why some companies make the leap . . . and others don't.* New York, NY: Harper Business.

Crites, S., Reed, C., & Runge, S. (2017, October). *Do I want to go to the dark side? A leadership capacity building program in a college of education and human services.* Paper presented at the meeting of the Teacher Education Council of State Colleges and Universities (TECSCU), Philadelphia, PA.

Dunning, D. (2017, November 9). *Why Incompetent People Think They're Amazing: An Animated Lesson from David Dunning* [TED Ed]. Retrieved from https://www.youtube.com/watch?v=pOLmD_WVY-E

Fullan, M., & Scott, G. (2009). *Turnaround leadership for higher education.* San Francisco, CA: Jossey-Bass.

Gmelch, W., & Buller, J. (2015). *Building academic leadership capacity: A guide to best practices.* San Francisco, CA: Jossey-Bass.

Goleman, D. (2017). *What makes a leader?* Boston, MA: Harvard Business Review Press. Gunsalus, C.K. (2011). *Basic guidelines for handing complaints [PDF file].* Madison, WI: Magna Publications. Retrieved from https://www.bcit.ca/files/judicial/pdf/complaint_handling/basic_guidelines_for_handling_complaints.pdf

Sinek, S.. (2014, May 19). *Why good leaders make you feel safe—Simon Sinek* [TED Talk]. Retrieved from https://youtu.be/lmyZMtPVodo

4

Simplify Whenever Possible

Great leaders are almost always great simplifiers, who can cut through argument, debate, and doubt to offer a solution everybody can understand.
—General Colin Powell

BIG IDEA FOR THIS CHAPTER

Given the organizational structures of modern universities and the bureaucracy that comes with colleges of education, I found that a necessary strategy for leading during my first year as a dean was to simplify the way we did things in the college. It was a default position and statement during my first year. I would ask, "What can we do to simplify this problem, issue, or system? Is there a simpler way to do this?" Most of the time, the answer was yes.

BIG IDEA

I have yet to meet the person who wants a more complicated, more confusing workplace. And yet, modern universities and colleges are complex and confusing places (Labaree, 2017). Ask any new person how things are going. Most of the time, you will get a pat answer that "Everything is fine" or "Things are going great." If you follow up on this question and dig a little deeper, we will notice that "how we do things" isn't as clear as we think it is. All it takes to get to this realization is two or three follow up questions. That might be our new measuring stick for organizational clarity: How well do our new people adjust to the ways and rhythms of our organization? This is more than simply being confused because you are the new guy. I have been the new guy four or five times in my career, and there is a continuum of support for people being brought into the organization. For our faculty and staff, it is our responsibility, whenever possible, to simplify the way our organizations work. Most universities have several key functions: teaching, research, service, and outreach to the greater community. Do our current ways of performing these functions have aspects that are counterproductive to the overall mission of the university? What is the simplest way to accomplish these goals?

Talking about simplifying the way we do things sounds, well, simple. It should be something that we able to spot and correct. But, it isn't usually that easy. Our environments become given, common sense, and accepted. The habits we have for getting things done within our colleges are, at the end of the day, the habits we are left with. They might not be the best, but they are the ones we have. Oftentimes, it is when we hire new people into our organizations that we hear someone say, "Why don't we do this, this way?" I have seen this in every leadership position that I have had. Sometimes the person asking this question is wrong. There is no other way to do the thing they are talking about. There is some regulation or policy from higher up that determines how we perform an action. In these cases, we have an explanation for why something looks the way that it does. In other cases (and this is much more common), there are other ways to do things. There aren't regulations or policies from higher up that determine how we perform an action. We have just decided to do it that way. In these cases, the responsibility is on us to make it better. Some people will be attached to the old way of doing things, and that's to be expected. We are all tied to things that are not the most efficient. We like it because it's what we know. It's comfortable, known, and routine—even if it's not the best way to do something.

In my experiences, changing the way that a task is performed most often falls into the structural frame (Chapter 2). There is usually something about the problem that is organizational in nature—something that deals with procedures, structures, policies, or responsibilities. In these cases, changes to the procedures, structures, policies, or responsibilities helps us to make the performance of these tasks easier, better, simpler. But it doesn't stop there. Many times, improving our structures has a positive impact on the other three frames: human resources, political, and symbolic. It's never simply about structures because the structures impact the other frames. Simplifying how we do things within our colleges taps into the positive aspects of human resources (i.e., human needs and participation), political (i.e., bargaining and networking), and symbolic (i.e., ritual and culture). Finding simpler ways to do things frees us to do the important jobs we were hired to do. The days this is most obvious are the days when you leave the office and you feel like you haven't accomplished much. Those are the days in which you look at your calendar and say, "What did I get accomplished today?" In my experience, those days are ones in which you are fighting with inefficient ways of doing things. Have you had many of those types of days? When starting a new job this is bound to happen because you don't quite know how things work yet. Or, is it because the systems you are attempting to navigate are outdated and ill-fitting? It will take time to figure out which one it is, or if it's both. At any rate, having these sorts of days is bad for our organizations and the people that work in them. It is a waste of money, talent, and potential.

Distinguishing Between Things You Can Control and Things You Cannot Control

During my first year, I read Ryan Holiday and Stephen Hanselman's book, *The Daily Stoic* (2016). This book is a daily devotional that uses the ancient ideas behind Stoicism to help guide our day-to-day lives. This book became a part of my daily morning routine (Chapter 7). I would read a bit each day, and reflect on how ideas from Marcus Aurelius, Epictetus, and Seneca could help me as a leader. One of the basic ideas behind Stoicism is the idea that we should focus on and concern ourselves with things that we can actually control—making a distinction between things we can change and things we cannot. This sounds like a simple mind trick, but it is more difficult than it sounds. By focusing only on the things we can actually control, we filter out the noise and frustration of those things that are outside of our control. It allows us to focus. We have a finite number of hours in the day and energy to devote to our work. Wisdom is knowing what to focus on. In the context of leadership and simplifying, the connection is clear. Separate the aspects of your college that you have control over from the things you do not have control over. Focus on simplifying the former, learn to live with the latter. When was the last time your day was ruined or you felt overwhelmed by something at work? Was this something you could control? Or was this something outside of your control?

As a new dean, I was constantly looking for ways to simplify the environment in which people worked. I believe that this desire comes from my past experiences where I was tapped to lead a department from the beginning of my tenure as a new teacher and a new assistant professor in Alabama. In those experiences, I was simplifying my environment and my job out of necessity. There were simply too many things to do. In order to get things done, I had to streamline the way the department functioned. I didn't know this at the time, but something else happened when I simplified things. People liked their jobs more. This wasn't an explicit goal I was shooting for in the early days of those jobs, but it happened. How do I know this? People told me. They would remark on a change (not immediately, but after they saw that it was better), and how it made a difference for the better. As a dean, I intended to make this an intentional part of my role as a leader. Make changes to simplify the workplace because it helps people get work done and because it's good for people, psychologically. Shouldn't we want this? For people to enjoy coming to work? Of course. I want people to love coming to work, or at least like coming to work. Colleges and universities shouldn't be difficult places to navigate—for students, staff, and faculty. If they aren't easy places to navigate, it's because we have created structures that prevent it. If we have created these prohibitive structures, it's within our power to do away with them. The other part of this is financial—universities invest a lot of money when they bring on new faculty and onboard them into the university community. Once we have made the decision to bring someone in to our community, we should not only ensure that they are supported so they can have the best shot at success, we should create an environment where things are as basic and simple as possible.

Ron Friedman's book *The Best Place to Work* (2014) is instructive here. He provides "lessons" for creating workplaces that support human potential and the work that we do. Although this book is not about higher education or university life, these lessons are applicable to the idea of simplifying things.

Lesson 1: Psychological needs are at the heart of employee engagement. "Provide opportunities for them to experience autonomy, competence, and relatedness on a daily basis" (p. 270).

Lesson 2: Organizations are more successful when they address the limits of the mind and body. "Our brains have limited bandwidth, and when the cognitive resources we have are depleted . . . our mood sours and our performance slumps" (p. 270).

Lesson 3: Integrating work and family life improves the quality of both. "The future . . . lies in helping employees fuse their personal and professional lives in ways that position them to deliver their best work" (p. 270).

Simplify. Simplify. Simplify.

When confronted with trying to decide if something should be simplified (it almost always can), ask these questions:

1. Why are we doing it this way?
2. Can we do this in fewer steps?
3. Have we asked the faculty or the leadership team what they think?
4. Does this way help or hinder us to accomplish our overall mission of teaching, research, service, and outreach?

My starting point for most of these conversations was with my leadership team. I did this mostly out of convenience, (i.e., there were less of them than faculty and we met regularly). I also started with them because I wanted to push the responsibility for making changes down one level to the Dean's Council. The members of the Dean's Council had all been at the university for several years, and they were knowledgeable about the ways in which the college worked for students. By pushing the responsibility for decision making down to the leadership team, I was also modeling for the team how they should make decisions within their areas of influence. Many times, people are tapped for leadership positions because they are perceived as people who get things done, but this is often at great personal and psychological cost. They shoulder the burden of the entire unit, feel compelled to make all of the decisions, and adhere to a leader-follower model of leadership (Marquet, 2012). It was my hope that the members of the Dean's Council would allow the people within their subunits to own the work of the group. By handing over responsibility for the operations of the group, the dynamics between the leader and the followers shifts. Amazing things happen when you ask the group, "Is there a better way to do this?" Once people get over the initial shock of being asked their opinion, they tell you what you need to hear. As leaders, we need to listen.

Another component of asking this question is the ability to let go of control. I have met many leaders in higher education who have a problem allowing other people to make decisions. This applies to small and big decisions alike. They come to this stance from a place of wanting to do the right things for the people they are leading. They want to ensure that it gets done, and that it's done right. How do I know this? Because this is literally what they say. These exact words:

1. I will just do it myself.
   (READ: Only I possess the skills to do this job.)
2. They will just mess it up, and I'll have to go behind them and fix it. It's just easier to do it myself. (extended version of #1)
   (READ: Only I have the skills to do this job, and I am saving myself time.)
3. I have to do it because they (followers) don't know how.
   (READ: The people I lead are ignorant and/or incompetent. They are not teachable.)

As the leader of a department or college, ask yourself what your default positions are here. What is your starting point? Do you see your people as helpless, incompetent followers, or do you see them as partners in accomplishing the goals of your unit? Your default positions might be:

1. I will delegate this to the appropriate person with the appropriate knowledge because I trust them to get the job done.
2. If they mess it up, I will coach/instruct them to do it correctly and have them try again.
3. If people don't know how to do something, I will ensure that they do know. Also, as the leader, it might be your fault that they don't know how. Tell them how.

It is not surprising that people like doing things the way they know how. Knowing how to do something is comforting to people; not knowing how to do something is uncomfortable. Intuitively, we know this to be true. If you have ever been the new person at a job, you know the feeling. There is a space between your knowledge of how things operate, and the expectations of the job. As you spend more time learning on the job, this space and the associated anxiety about not knowing goes away. This is the irony of trying to simplify aspects of your organization as a leader. People often prefer their way of doing things, even if it makes sense to do it in another way. Sometimes people immediately see that their way is inefficient, but sometimes they do not. How you address these conversations goes a lot way in determining whether or not the change will happen.

This interaction often follows a familiar pattern. You ask someone within the organization why we do something in a particular way, pointing out weaknesses or inefficiencies. Then you suggest a change or new way forward. This is followed by people telling you why we can't do it that way. They will explain why this is the case by giving you a history of the issue, who was involved in making this decision, and who will be impacted if the change is made. They are telling you it can't be done and whom it will impact because they believe this to be true. They have come to think of this way of doing this task as the only way it can be accomplished. Of course, this is rarely the truth. There are other ways to do things, and the impact on others isn't always as catastrophic as people assume it will be. We often imagine the worst-case scenario of what change will be like. It can be uncomfortable, for sure, but catastrophic? Almost never. As the leader, one of our responsibilities in these sorts of interactions is to help the person (or group) understand that their way isn't the only way to do something. A simple "why?" or "why not?" goes a long way in these discussions.

> **Faculty member:** We can't do X that way because of Y.
>
> **Leader:** Why not? What if we changed this, and moved this here? Wouldn't this work better?
>
> **Faculty member:** Well, the reason we do it this way is because of A, B, and C.

In my career, I have noticed that A, B, and C aren't as ironclad as the person thinks they are. We overcomplicate things by assuming that A, B, and C are immoveable and non-negotiable. We can change the arrangements of things in our organizations. We want to solicit feedback (that's where the Dean's Council comes in), and we want to listen, but our arrangements are things we have created. Since these arrangements are our creations, then we simply need to recreate/revise/rethink these arrangements to better suit our work. As responsibility flows from the leader down to other leaders within the college, a funny thing begins to happen. The mindset of people changes from one in which systems are controlling them, to them controlling the systems. The culture shifts from complaining about our problems to a mindset that we can simply change the way we do things to address our problems. Complaining about problems or fixing problems? This is an easy decision.

Creating Conditions Where People Can Do Good Work

In Chapter 1 I wrote that I believe that a dean's primary role is to create conditions where people can do good work. This idea and how it plays out will be a function of the context of your leadership role. Colleges and universities all have a distinctive culture, and that plays a major part of trying to create conditions. If you have ever worked at more than one university, the differences in cultures can be quite striking.

Creating this environment inevitably involves making changes to the current structure. There is a continuum of readiness within colleges (see

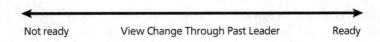

Figure 4.1 Continuum of readiness when considering change.

Figure 4.1). On one end we have people who are not ready for change. At all. They are people who are comfortable with the way things currently operate, even if they realize intuitively that things could be better. Learning new ways takes time and effort, and frankly, they don't see that it's worth it. There is another group that sees ideas for change almost exclusively through an historical lens. They see change and attempts at change against a backdrop of former leadership and the ways in which they led the college. I have seen this play out at multiple universities. This version of resistance is directly proportional to the popularity of the previous leader. The more the former leader was liked by the college, the harder it is to make changes, the less the former leader was liked, the easier it is to make changes. On the other end of the spectrum we have people who are ready for change, early adopters if you will. These are the people who recognized before you arrived that things should and could be different, but weren't given the authority or space to make necessary changes.

The point of this is that change is situational, contextual, and leader specific. What works in one situation won't necessarily work in another (Sample, 2002). Along this continuum, where do your faculty currently see themselves? Where do you see them? Do faculty see themselves as change agents, or do they see themselves as workers who just do what they are told? If the environment supports the latter, you and your college are missing out on the talents and good ideas of your faculty.

Change is Hard and Taking the Long View

Most of the changes we attempted to make in year one were in response to problems or days in which I felt bogged down by the bureaucracy of doing things the same way. As I have already noted, simplifying the ways in which tasks are completed or the ways in which work is done is about more than "making things easier," although this is a definite side effect. Simplifying your unit or organization takes some courage, and courage isn't always the easiest thing to muster. It takes courage as a leader to implement change, and it takes courage from faculty to make changes. We are asking people to leave aspects of their jobs that are known, comfortable, and routine and to replace it with unknown, uncomfortable, and new. Never forget this aspect of being a new leader and the process of change. Even in cases in which you have people in favor of your ideas for change, you will always have some who won't like it. It doesn't mean that they are bad people or that they want you to fail in your efforts. Change is hard for people within organizations for one simple reason: when you change things, someone loses (Heifetz, 1994). In cases of reorganization, people are losing their work identity, but even with small shifts and changes within an organization, people are losing the knowledge about how to do things. This alone—ignorance about how to do things in the organization—can be a pretty scary thing for most people.

Keep this at the forefront of your mind when making changes the first year. The best-case scenario for making changes, whether it's your first year or not, is to make sure that the faculty is involved in the changes. It could be that the idea for the change comes directly from them, but at the very least, make sure that they are involved in the changes. Of course, the process I am describing is an ideal state. This is how you'd like to do things in a perfect world under positive conditions. There will be times when you, as the leader, won't quite make changes as you should, or consult with the right people, or even make the right decisions. Getting this wrong, on occasion, is a part of leadership. Getting to simpler ways of doing things requires more than just cutting things out. As the examples below illustrate, simplifying things takes work. When we take something away we are forced to rethink how we do things, which is a process in and of itself. That was the most difficult hurdle I faced my first year when implementing change. I view the ideas in this chapter as process oriented—it's not one move, but several moves coordinated to work in tandem with other moves. I also view these ideas and examples as taking the long view. Taking the long view assumes that these changes are being made and processes are being simplified not for today or tomorrow, but for a month and a year from now. I was not looking for immediate change for change's sake. I was looking for gradual change, over time, to improve how we support the mission of the college. These aren't quick fixes because the culture of a college can't be changed or "fixed" overnight. Some people see that last sentence as bad news. The idea that we can't change things overnight and have smooth sailing for the rest of our time at an institution almost sounds like we are powerless. But, remember this: the ways that a college or organization do things is itself a process that has evolved over time. Cultures and rituals evolved in your particular context over the course of years across several leaders with different faculty. You are the next link in the chain. If it has taken time to get to the current state of affairs, it is going to take some time to reverse course where necessary. Be patient in this process.

Ways We Simplified Things During My First Year

Forms

As I mentioned before, in colleges of education, a big part of what we do includes working with local school districts to place our students for their fieldwork and internships. One of the ways we simplified in this area was to move to electronic forms whenever possible. This one sounds like common sense, but it is more than just going from paper versions to electronic versions. It also involves how we get information to students, how forms are collected, and how required documentation is submitted. We found that all aspects of our internship placement process were improved by defaulting to electronic communication with our forms. This applied to the students who would be doing their internships as well as the schools that we partnered with for this part of our programs. Google Forms and Google Documents were a welcome change to the people who worked in this office.

Internships

This one is related to forms. One of the first things that I wanted to learn about as the new dean was how and where we placed our students for their internships. Most colleges of education have formal agreements with local school districts in which the college requests that the local schools host students for their student teaching. That much was clear. Why we used particular districts was less clear. When I asked how many school districts we used to place students, the response was 14. This meant that we had to maintain positive relationships, communicate with, and support our students across 14 different school districts. Fourteen districts is fine, if you have the capacity to maintain these relationships. Our college of education was smaller than most, and I did not feel that we should be stretched this thin. In my mind, fewer but stronger relationships would be better than our current set up. The other aspect of this is logistics. Placing interns in schools is a very time intensive exercise. Colleges of education must consider the needs of the intern, the fit of the school with the appropriate subject, travel of faculty and supervisors to the school, and a host of other issues. In consultation with my director, we decided to reduce the number of school districts from 14 to six. This allowed us to focus on fewer school districts, which allowed us to strengthen the ways in which we partnered with these schools. The major disagreement with this change was that it was different from the way they had done things in the past. By the end of the first year of having fewer districts, it was clear that we had made the right decision. At the close of the academic year, we were approached by Education First (https://education-first.com) to collaborate on a "Teacher Prep Partnerships Toolkit." We worked with this group to develop a short case study on our partnership and will be featured in a forthcoming publication from Education First. In our work with the school district, the strategic placement of student teachers with the best mentor teachers was emphasized. This would not have been possible under our former system. In this case, less was definitely more.

Scheduling: Schedules can be a bureaucratic mess. Anyone who has served as chair or associate dean knows this to be true. When I served as associate director in Ohio, I remember hearing faculty and program coordinators complain about how difficult it was to create and submit semester schedules. It seemed to me that the different programs were struggling with the same issues, but that no one was talking to one another. So I invited the program coordinators, our advisors, and field placement coordinators to a meeting to discuss why they were having such problems creating the schedule. One hour later it was clear: there were too many people involved in making the schedule to not have discussions about how it should look. They were creating schedules that satisfied their needs and their students' needs without regard for other programs. By meeting and talking through common issues, we greatly improved the way we developed the schedule. The other thing that I introduced in Ohio, and as a new dean, was a standard protocol and form. The protocol directed the responsible parties to a particular due date (every term), and the form ensured that everyone was seeing the same information in the same format. Prior to implementing these two changes, schedules from the different departments and programs were just that—different. With a standard form and protocol, we were all on the same page (literally). This form also assisted the administrative assistants who were responsible for inputting the schedule into the system. Win for the professors creating the schedule. Win for the assistants responsible for inputting the schedule. Win for the students who got a schedule that met their needs. It only took one meeting. Win.

Committees

Committees within colleges and universities do not have a good reputation. I have literally never heard someone say, "I love doing committee work. It is the reason I come to work." There is a tension in the culture of universities that pits the idea of self-governance against good teaching and scholarship. I think this is an oversimplification, but it does bear some truth. I know this because I have served on many committees during my time in higher education. This tension is founded on the perception that dull, useless committee work takes time away from the real reasons that people aspire to work in higher education: teaching, learning, writing, thinking. Another part of this is that many faculty only have vague notions of what specific committees are actually responsible for accomplishing. One of the things that we did in my first year was to examine current committees and look for committees that weren't useful to the operations of the college. Almost immediately the faculty decided to get rid of some committees and combine others. One other thing that I plan to do during my second year is to develop a list of current committees, their membership, charges, and other important information. This should help with faculty uncertainty about what a committee is responsible for accomplishing.

Curriculum Maps

For some of you, the following description will sound like the opposite of simplifying things within a college. This example is one in which a little bit of work to set up a system makes the operation of the program or department simpler because you have an idea of what is being done and where it's being done. Colleges of education are held to very high and very specific accreditation standards. One of the things that colleges of education are known for (for better or worse) is the idea of teaching potential teachers with national and state standards as a focus of our programs. To this end, we must know when a standard is taught and in what class. Our accrediting agency demands that we monitor how we "know" that our students have been exposed to and have met these standards. As the new dean, I asked, "How do we know which standards are being met in which classes?" The response? Shoulder shrugs. Most people within programs did not know what people in their program were doing in their classes. We needed a document that mapped out what standards were being met in which classes. We needed a curriculum map (see Simpson Assessment's (2013) video https://www.youtube.com/watch?v=TjnQzF2M-iE for a brief overview). This allows the members of a department or program to see what concepts are being covered and taught, so they can ensure that their classes align with program requirements. I was lucky that one of my department chairs, who had been a school principal in California earlier in her career, had extensive experience with curriculum mapping. Our college was able to map the curricula from all of our programs within that first year because of her leadership in this area. Once one program completed their "map" and shared with the rest of the faculty, it became clear that this was needed across the college. Yes, it required work on the front end, but it will help simplify the ways in which we think about course sequencing and accreditation efforts moving forward.

Data Retreat

It was tradition in my college to have a data retreat at the beginning of the year. This is a great way to look back at the previous year to see where improvements can be made to the ways that we deliver our programs. For colleges of education, this is a chance to look at the data that is collected on our teacher candidates, their performance in the field, job placement rates, their test scores, and a host of other indicators that we collect for accreditation purposes. Faculty are also grouped by program so they can look at the data from their program. This allows them to make data informed decisions about program improvements. I am glad that our college already has a history of doing a yearly data retreat because I believe that it is a necessary component of accreditation and continuous improvement efforts. The feelings of the faculty, however, were different. Although they could see the inherent value of having a data retreat, there were some parts of the retreat that they told me they wanted to change. And, by change, they were requesting that it be simplified. With feedback from the leadership team and program faculty, we made changes. First, we cut the retreat from an all-day meeting with lunch, to a half-day meeting with a "working lunch." Most people were finished by 12:30 or 1:00. Second, we structured the day where many people were allowed to talk and present data to the group. Having one speaker can be a more efficient way to deliver information; but it's not a good way to conduct a half-day retreat. Third, we segmented the morning into time slots where programs could work together on examining their data. Last, we made sure that the programs were able to set goals for the upcoming year. Did the faculty leave that retreat with a greater appreciation for the importance of data analysis and accreditation? I'm not sure. But we accomplished what we needed to accomplish in less time.

Appeals Processes

In our college, students are allowed to appeal decisions that pertain to admission and internship. These decisions were based on having the appropriate GPA and having passed entrance exams. We had appeals processes for people who weren't quite at the level that they needed to be. Appeals were granted very rarely for admission to the program. For admission to internship, which was the last stage of the program before graduation, appeals were never granted. We had an appeals process that gave students false hope that they would be allowed to progress to the next step because they were never granted. This drained time from the faculty serving on the committee and made students jump through hoops with no indication that they would get their appeal granted. So, we decided to do away with this level of appeal.

Repeat Yourself, Often

When it comes to simplifying your college's operations and changing the ways you do things, don't expect change to occur overnight. I have experienced this as a coach, teacher, professor, and an administrator. You have clear reasons for making the changes you make, you explain it in the clearest language you can think of, you ask people if they understand, they nod and say that they do. Voilà. The changes are made. Not quite. Traditions and routines, no matter how inefficient are hard to replace. I will admit that this was one of the most frustrating parts of being a new dean and trying to implement simpler, more efficient ways of conducting business. The truth is that we all struggle with change, and your faculty and staff will struggle with this as well. The answer to this is twofold: patience and repeating your message (Marquet, 2012). I tried to simplify whenever I could, but I also was trying to push the responsibility for making these changes function to lower levels of the college. It wasn't that the dean was changing things and the rest of the college would blindly follow my direction. Rather, it was chair led or professor led or staff led changes that I wanted. But, old habits die hard. I got to the point where I was repeating myself so much that I was beginning to wonder if I was getting on people's nerves. I kept prefacing my comments with "I know you have heard me say this before, but..."

David Marquet writes about this in his book *Turn the Ship Around: A True Story of Turning Followers into Leaders* (2012). He was struggling with getting the men aboard his submarine to think of themselves as leaders with roles to play. Marquet reminds us that "REPEATING THE MESSAGE is a mechanism for COMPETENCE" (p. 149).

> Repeat the same message day after day, meeting after meeting, event after event. Sounds redundant, repetitive, and boring. But what's the alternative? Changing the message? That results in confusion and a lack of direction. I didn't realize the degree to which old habits die hard, even when people are emotionally on board with the change... They just pictured something from their past. It was hard for them to create an image of what we were trying to accomplish. It was something brand new." (p. 150)

During my first year as dean, this was something that I had to work on, but it was worth it. Consistent messaging about the things you want to accomplish. Consistent messaging about simplifying the way your college operates should be a daily message in your conversations with your staff and faculty. Defaulting to the simpler ways of doing things helps us (collectively) to get out of our own way so we can accomplish what we are here to do: teach, learn, research, write, and serve. There's no reason we have to make this harder than it has to be. We are responsible for the roadblocks that prevent us from doing these things. We have seen the enemy, and he is us. Therefore, we need to get rid of the roadblocks. Simplifying does just that.

_____

References

Friedman, R. (2014). *The best place to work: The art and science of creating an extraordinary workplace.* New York, NY: Perigee Books.

Heifetz, R. (1994). *Leadership without easy answers.* Cambridge, MA: Harvard University Press.

Holiday, R., & Hanselman, S. (2016). *The daily stoic: 366 meditations on wisdom, perseverance, and the art of living.* New York, NY: Random House.

Labaree, D. F. (2017). *A perfect mess: The unlikely ascendancy of American higher education.* Chicago, IL: University of Chicago Press.

Marquet, L. D. (2012). *Turn the ship around! A true story of turning followers into leaders.* New York, NY: Penguin Press.

Sample, S. (2002). *The contrarian's guide to leadership.* San Francisco, CA: Jossey-Bass.

[Simpson Assessment]. (2013, November). Curriculum Mapping [Video File]. Retrieved from https://www.youtube.com/watch?v=TjnQzF2M-iE

5

Be Radical

A leader is best when people barely know he exists, when his work is done,
his aim fulfilled, they will say: we did it ourselves.

—Lao Tzu

BIG IDEA FOR THIS CHAPTER

During my first year, there were so many things that vied for my attention; there was a struggle to focus on the root of cause of things. This is what I mean when I say "be radical." Radical means "going to the root" of things. This means ignoring the noise (and there is a lot some days) and focusing on the things that matter. As a new dean, you are asked to make decisions as if you already possessed adequate knowledge to do so. This isn't always the case. With this in mind, I suggest being radical in two areas: your own knowledge base (what you know about the institution) and your people. This is the foundation of your day-to-day existence as a dean: having technical knowledge of the college you lead and working with your people.

The term *radical* has several connotations. Most of them deal with someone being radical in the sense of being outside the box of normal conventions. You are a political radical or you are suggesting a radical change to some existing social arrangement. Below are some definitions (Oxford Living Dictionary, n.d.) for the word radical:

1. Relating to or affecting the fundamental nature of something; far-reaching or thorough.
2. Advocating or based on thorough or complete political or social change; representing or supporting an extreme or progressive section of a political party.

The aspect of the word radical that I think fits nicely with thinking about our roles as leaders is in the origin of the word. The origin is from the late Latin word radicalis and from Latin radix meaning "forming the root" and "inherent." With this in mind, what are the essential components of your day that form the root of what you do? I also think of the idea of literal roots when thinking about leadership. When I was growing up in rural Alabama, I remember oak trees in our backyard. These massive trees were held upright and were sustained by a network of roots that were mostly underground and out of sight. But they were there the whole time, ensuring that the tree would survive. This is how I think of the word radical and its application to leadership.

What are the roots that sustain you? For me, it was having a basic knowledge of the college so that I could contextualize all of the information, decisions, and demands that came my way on a daily basis. I needed to learn more about the college. Some of this learning happens automatically. You hear a term or label for something in a meeting, and then you hear it again, and eventually you figure out what it means. This way of learning, although appropriate and normal, was not cutting it for me during my first year. This form of learning was simply too slow. Below I discuss how I sped up that process. The other root that I discuss is the people in your college. More than your technical knowledge about the college, the people with whom you work sustain your efforts as a leader. Put your people first, and the rest will fall in to place. Actually, that's oversimplifying things. It's more like: put your people first, and they will be more likely to do the right things for the organization.

The Shift from Unknown Unknowns to Known Unknowns

The first semester of my deanship was very much a semester of unknown unknowns. By this I mean that things were unknown to me and because I was new, I didn't even know that these things were unknown to me. I simply didn't know what I didn't know. This wasn't from a lack of trying. I was trying to learn. But, I couldn't differentiate between the really important things I was hearing, and the not so important things I was hearing. Eventually, I would need to know both—important and not so important—but the first semester I tried to pick up on the most important things. It was a sort of a knowledge triage. When you are the new person, everything is new. In meetings with faculty or other administrators, it was very common for me to lean over to the person sitting beside me and ask, "What are they talking about" or "What does that acronym stand for?" From this perspective, being a new dean requires that you become comfortable with ambiguity and a certain level of not knowing. Because it is my habit to get out of the office whenever I can, I walk the halls of my building on a pretty regular basis. Usually, every hour I leave the office and walk the halls. I used this routine to stop and ask people questions about things in the college. I remember thinking that I was asking a lot of questions.

During this time frame, that was my learning pattern. I would go to people in the college and ask questions about their areas. This method filled in many of the blanks in my knowledge base. The problem with this approach is that it was based on my questioning. Because there was so much I didn't know, the answers and knowledge I was getting were limited by my questions. You get answers to the questions you ask. I was, many times, asking limited questions, therefore I was getting limited answers. Even if I had been asking all of the right questions, the amount of information needed to run a college is so overwhelming, I couldn't have retained or processed it anyways. It's simply too much.

Around January, there began a shift in my thinking and my technical knowledge base about the college. Although there were many things that I still didn't know about the university and the college, I began to realize and see what I didn't know (known unknowns). I was no longer in the "I don't know what I don't know" area. I was beginning to realize the things that I didn't know. I began to notice that I did know what I didn't know. I could make out an outline of the ecosystems that existed in the college. How things fit together, and how things are related. In the first semester, I spent my time going from person to person asking questions in a rather haphazard fashion. This was good for the first term, but not efficient. In hindsight, I now see that I was essentially asking questions to get through the day. In terms of my own learning, it was the equivalent of being a teacher and staying one day ahead of the students. Because I was beginning to learn how the college operated, I wondered how I could accelerate this process, become more aware of things, and stop being so reactive to my own learning. I needed a plan. The plan I developed is painfully simple, but it worked. For the reader, what follows may border on the absurd because it seems so simple, that the ideas on the next couple of pages are common sense. Perhaps they are, perhaps they aren't. I share them with the reader as an example of simplifying learning and going to the root of learning about your unit. This process and idea unfolded for me the week I realized I was beginning to feel a bit more comfortable in my own understanding and knowledge of the college. I don't think this would've worked as well in the early parts of that first year because I was getting acclimated to the job and I was already being bombarded with information, meetings, and demands of being the new guy. My plan was simple: index cards and briefings.

Index Cards

This idea hit me on a random Tuesday morning. If I wanted to learn about the college from a position of knowing what I didn't know, I'd have to do it the way I did in other settings. I would study. I would study the college like I would study any other content or idea. I would devote time to collecting information, reading it, and studying it. I remember the day that it happened. I asked my administrative assistant if we had any note cards in our office supplies. We did, and she brought me a partial set of index cards. Next, from memory and on a sheet of paper, I wrote as many terms as I could think of. Some of these where terms that I understood and could talk about, others not so much. It was an exercise in dumping the knowledge I had collected that first semester into a list of terms. The list was surprisingly easy to make, which is one of the points of this exercise. I had a list of over 250 terms, only half of which I actually felt comfortable saying that I understood or was knowledgeable about. I was, for the first time, aware of what I didn't know (or at least acknowledged what I needed to learn). I used this list to create a list of index cards to study—just like a freshman studying for a midterm. The term on one side, the information on the other.

I spent the next couple weeks filling out my cards. Some I could fill out from my preliminary knowledge; other cards I had to seek out the knowledge. In the latter, I would often email the person and ask, "What are the five most important things about your program/office/area?" I would then write these things as bullet points on the index card. For other items I would do a search on the university website or state department of education. When I was all said and done, I had over 300 index cards to study. These cards were always with me.

Once I learned the material on these cards, it allowed me to listen with context and a basic knowledge of terms and concepts within the university.

These cards did not give me deep knowledge, but they did allow me a knowledge that allowed deep knowledge to take root. It allowed me to listen to people speak in meetings from a baseline of information that I did not have before. I was able to, in a real sense, enter into conversations for the first time. Creating these index cards allowed me to learn information about being a dean at this institution in a way that I am not sure could have been accomplished any other way. Sure, I could have waited to figure things out through just hearing things over and over, but that would've taken too long.

As the dean, you are expected to make decisions and direct people in the right ways. This is virtually impossible without the sort of baseline informational knowledge that I am describing. Doing this exercise is about being intentional with your learning. It's about saying to yourself, "I need to know more about that. I need to commit to learning it, so I can do my job better." I believe that it also takes a degree of humility to admit that you need to return to that basic sort of studying that you did when you were an undergraduate student studying for midterms. It takes a moment of clarity in which you realize that you need to do something different to accelerate the learning necessary to run the college. I made an effort to study the cards once in the morning and once in the evening. Sometimes this was more focused than other times. For some sessions, it was a quick read through; other times it was a concentrated study session in which I tried to commit the terms to memory. Over time, like anything else, working on this a little each day paid off. It paid off in ways that were unexpected. I noticed that I didn't have as many questions for the people in my college. On second thought, I take that back. I did have questions, as I did before, but the nature of the questions was different. There were less content/informational questions, and more analytical/synthesis questions. This was, in my mind, proof of my development and learning. Creating and studying index cards did the trick. Basic. Simple. Old school. A pen, some note cards, and study time. Studying things so that you know what they are called, where they are located, who it impacts. Confidence follows.

Briefings

The quieter you become, the more you hear.

—Rumi

I cannot overestimate the positive impact that studying index cards had on my first year as a dean. I realize that the previous sentence sounds sort of silly, but it's true. The basic truth is that I had rediscovered a way to accelerate learning basic knowledge about the way the college worked, and this helped me be more confident and more informed in my daily roles as dean. I went from being uncertain about things being said in meetings to actually knowing what people were talking about. If you have ever been the new person at a university, you know exactly what I am describing. It's like everyone in the room is speaking a different language. I can remember the first time that I attended a meeting of the deans with the provost at his "Provost Council" meeting. I liken it to an episode of any of the popular TV shows about doctors who work at a hospital (e.g., *ER*, *Grey's Anatomy*). Predictably during the show, a patient comes into the hospital needing treatment, and the doctors spring into action. During this process, they all use technical language required to help the patient. They throw around highly specialized language pertinent to the field of medicine. As a viewer, you are less concerned with the language they are using than you are with the status of the character in the story, but you notice the words they are using. If for no other reason, you recognize it because it sounds foreign to you. This was how I felt at those first meetings.

The same week that I decided to create index cards to help with my learning, I also made another decision. It dawned on me that the different parts of the college were operating mostly independent of the dean's office. This isn't to say that they were doing a bad job. Quite the contrary. They were doing a pretty good job. From where I was sitting, I didn't feel that I understood all of what was occurring in the different parts of the college. I had a vague idea of who was leading the different areas, and the big ideas behind their work, but I lacked specifics on what was happening in these different areas. So I decided to have monthly "briefings." Again, to the reader, this idea probably sounds common sense and obvious, but this sort of structured protocol was not in place in this college before my arrival. The idea is simple. I would schedule monthly, 30-minute meetings with the faculty and staff who were leaders in the different offices in the college. There was one key difference in this idea from the way I had been doing things the first semester—the information would flow in the other direction. Instead of me asking them questions about what they were doing, they would come to me and give reports on their units. Below is the email that I sent out in mid-January. There is a description of what I wanted followed by the schedule of meetings. The schedule of appointments is organized by subunit (there are 12 in my college); I scheduled three of these meetings per week. Below the schedule, I provided the subunits with a template of what I'd like them to discuss. This would allow me to file their briefs away and refer to them the next time we met.

COE Leaders,

If you are receiving this email, you are a leader of one of the areas/units in the COE. During my first semester, I spent a lot of time learning how things work in the College, but it was superficial learning. I picked up on terms, people associated with parts of the college, programs, etc., but not much in the way of depth of understanding.

That's where the idea of briefings comes in. The idea is simple. I want you to set up meetings with me for 25–30 minutes, once a month. When you meet with me, I'd like for you to report on the issues in your area. It will be a time where we can discuss issues, problem solve, and share information. It will also help me to better understand the intricacies of the area you are leading. I'd like to meet with three of you each week, so I am assigning you a week (each month) that I'd like to meet. See table below.

Please make an appointment with Theresa to get on my calendar.

First Week of the Month	Second Week of the Month	Third Week of the Month	Fourth Week of the Month
Department Chair	Department Chair	Associate Dean	Director of Teacher Ed
Licensure Officer	Graduate Coordinator 1	Graduate Coordinator 2	Center for Rural Education
STEM Center	CAEP (accreditation)	General Studies	Academic Partnerships

When we meet, I'd like for you to bring me a short, written "brief." This will guide our discussions.

Your brief should follow the template below (also attached).

1. Name and Program or Area
2. What are you working on?
3. What successes are you having?
4. What problems are you having?
5. Are there things I need to know about?
6. What are the numbers in your area?
7. Anything else you want to discuss.
   (Personal communication, February 9, 2018)

Having these briefing meetings was one of the best things that I established during my first year. I found that the people who were leading the different parts of the college were eager to share what they were doing and talk with me about solving problems. As I was thinking of implementing this idea, I wrote out several different drafts of an email and different ways to organize the meetings. Although I believe that I decided on the simplest format, one thing became clear. And it's clear to me as I write this sentence. There are many moving parts in a college of education—department chairs, leaders of college centers, accreditation people, graduate coordinators, and faculty who coordinate external academic services. The range and variety of tasks that these people perform can be overwhelming. It's complicated. I can attest to this feeling. I felt overwhelmed in trying to learn the ins and outs of all that they did for the college. I truly believe that this feeling of being overwhelmed was diminished by my use of index cards and monthly briefings. Here are the main takeaways, for me as a new dean, in doing these activities:

Your default position is that of a learner: Most people come to the deanship as successful, tenured professors. We are used to being "experts" in our classrooms and when discussing our subject area. The existence of being a professor is wrapped up in knowing a lot about your area. The courses we teach, the papers we write, and the talks we give at conferences are a testament to our specialized knowledge in an area. Although I believe that being a professor is about learning more and more about your area of expertise, the bulk of your job consists of knowing about your subject. Being a new dean at a new university is completely the opposite. You are a novice again. This can be a shock to a person who is used to knowing "everything" about a topic. In this context, your default position and stance should shift from being an expert to being a student. This requires a sense of curiosity about how things at your college work. There is a simple test to see if you are approaching your new job as an expert (which doesn't help you much in your new role) or as a student (who needs to learn). Which do you do more often: make statements/pronouncements or ask questions? If you ask more questions, there's a good chance that you are taking this "curious student" role seriously.

Pace yourself: The process I am describing takes time and effort. Lots of time and lots of effort. As I have stated above, it took me an entire semester to see the faint outlines of how the pieces of the college fit together. Learning the specifics about how the college worked took another eight months. The slowness of this process is not a testament to your lack of abilities to learn quickly, but rather it is the result of the complexity of colleges in general. That's what index cards and briefing meetings do. They help us to learn and digest this information in smaller chunks. They organize the complex into simpler, manageable bites.

Let people talk about their work: Once I started having my briefings, another thing became clear. People are glad to talk about the work that they are doing. They are proud of their accomplishments and how they represent the college's many parts. I believe that this is something we should tap in to more often. Go to the source to learn about the successes and struggles that they are having. Allow them the space to talk through these issues, and help them solve problems. Listen. Listen some more. And, then assist.

Orientation as a "Founder"

Over the years when I have looked at job opportunities on the Chronicle of Higher Education or higheredjobs.com, I have noticed the title of "Founding Dean." It's a job in which the person they are looking for will be responsible for building or creating a college or unit where one hasn't existed before. You are literally the "founder" of that college. Predictably, when universities write the job descriptions for these sorts of jobs, they are looking for candidates with a certain skill set and experiences. The job announcement makes it clear that they are looking for someone with a wide range of experiences who can create something new. The language used to describe the position and the person they are looking for speaks to the developmental nature of the job. Most are intentional in the ways they describe the job where structures will have to be built, relationships will need to be fostered and solidified, and programs will be created. It is clear that being a "Founding Dean" contains struggles and birth pangs related to creating things where they don't exist. The logic is simple: creating new things where they don't exist is harder than monitoring and supervising things that already exist. Below is sample text from a Founding Dean job opening I found in the spring of 2018. The university was looking for someone who would be good at:

- Collaboratively crafting the School's mission, vision, values, and strategic plan;
- Advancing the administrative structure to support future directions;
- Responding and contributing to important state and national priorities for education;
- Recruiting, retaining, and supporting a diverse faculty, staff, and student body;
- Enhancing existing and developing new academic programs;
- Generating and sustaining diverse revenue streams through program development/expansion, enrollment management, fundraising, and extramural support for research and scholarly activities;
- Candidates should possess the ability to develop and sustain strong external relationships with leaders from multiple sectors, including school districts, community organizations, public officials, foundations, and universities.

As with most job advertisements for deanships, this one seems overwhelming at first glance. But, founding deans have the added aspect of being someone who can not only lead change (which all deans have to do at some point), but also being someone who can create. At this point, you may be wondering how this idea of "founder" meshes with being a new dean.

During my first year, one of my biggest frustrations was that I often felt the college didn't have structures in place that I thought it should. This is common for deans. They come in to a new situation, and because they are new, they see issues and persistent problems from a new perspective. In many ways, new people can see things that people who have worked a place for years cannot see. It doesn't necessarily mean that the new people with the new perspectives are always right. It means that because they are not tied to traditional ways of doing things, they see things for what they are—good, bad, or somewhere in between. This was my experience during the first year. I was often frustrated because something didn't work quite like I thought it should. I also noticed that this perceived dysfunction was impacting the work experience of people in the college. It wasn't simply an annoyance because I didn't like something. It was more about the impact that these issues were having on morale and workplace environment.

And then one morning it hit me. I was on my morning jog and had a realization. My feelings of frustration were misplaced and unproductive. I had oriented myself in the wrong direction. The mistake I was making is one that, in hindsight, seems silly. I was approaching my job and my orientation to this job from the standpoint of the dean of a college with no problems. If you situate yourself as a dean of a college that has no problems, then you are going to be constantly frustrated when problems arise. For me, this was about my personal orientation and professional expectations. I was disoriented. I had unrealistic expectations. I was facing the wrong direction (Plato, 1992).

What if we, as new deans, oriented ourselves as "founders?" What if our default position was one of starting something new and expecting an uphill climb? I have always been someone who prefers to be given realistic expectations for a job or task that's before me. I prefer you tell me that it's going to be hard and that it will be a struggle. I have found that the first year of being a dean shares much in common with the job advertisements for founding deans. I found myself "creating" nearly every day. Surely deans who are tapped to be founding deans do not get frustrated when structures, protocols, and cultures aren't in place. That would be absurd—to be upset that something doesn't exist, when it's your job to create these things. This was a course correction that I had to make my first year. I had to shift from frustration to opportunity. Instead of being frustrated because we didn't have something, I needed to view things through the lens of being a founder. These weren't problems to be solved, they were opportunities to create new and better ways of doing things. This may sound like semantics or a mind trick that I am trying to play on myself, but it's not. We need to focus on the things we can change and pay attention to our perception of those things (Holiday, 2014). Thinking of yourself as a founder helps to lead the way. Do you expect there to be no problems? Do you see them as given? Founders don't expect problems; because they don't see problems. They see opportunities.

What is (Really) Happening Here?

A central part of "being radical" or getting to the root of things, is to actually understand what is happening. When I say understand what is happening, I mean to literally understand what is happening. This is harder than it sounds, especially as a new leader. There are two ideas from psychology that help us to understand why this seemingly simple idea (i.e., discerning what is happening) is, in reality, not simple at all. In fact, determining what is happening in a given context and what we should do next can sometimes seem impossible. It's difficult because of the ideas of confirmation bias and cognitive dissonance. There are many articles and videos online that detail these ideas (see Resources), but for our purposes, a simple sketch of each will suffice. The point here is to understand these concepts and to be aware that they are operating in you and the people you are attempting to lead. It doesn't mean that your faculty are dishonest or bad people; on the contrary, it means that your faculty are human beings. These systems are a part of the way our brains function. This is about awareness of these concepts.

First, confirmation bias is the tendency to see evidence that only supports your already existing belief systems. We see this in cable new shows, politics, even in sports. In short, the evidence that helps our side win (the argument or the game), is perceived by us as being "right." We are blinded by our own preconceived ideas. Literally. If you watch one of the major cable news channels, you know this to be right. Do you have one that you watch every night, or do you alternate between Fox News, CNN, and MS-NBC? My guess is that you have one that you watch to the exclusion of the others. You choose this one because it supports your already existing worldview. You choose it because it represents an echo chamber for your ideas. Secondly, there is the idea of cognitive dissonance. Dissonance occurs when we are confronted with information that clashes with our previously held positions on something. We have all experienced this emotion. You have strong opinions about a topic that you believe are obviously right and correct. Then someone comes along and tells you that you are wrong or that you are mistaken in your thinking. As the previous concept (confirmation bias) bears out, these aren't the sorts of conversations that we seek out. But cognitive dissonance is about those moments when this information visits us anyways. Now, let's assume that the person who has told you that you are wrong about a topic goes one step further. Not only do they tell you that you are incorrect about this issue, they actually bring you data and evidence to support their claim. What do most people do in this situation? Do we change our minds and thank the person who has just told us the truth—a truth that is in opposition to our strongly held belief? Cognitive science tells us that most people don't change their minds. In fact, not only do we not change our minds, we stick to our disproven position even more strongly than before. That's right. After we've been proven wrong (with evidence and data), we believe our position even more strongly than before we were proven incorrect. The person who brought you the truth has made it harder for you to actually see the truth.

In leading a college as a new dean, these two concepts are always operating. When you attempt to get to the root causes of issues and/or problems in your college, these cognitive structures are operating in the heads of people involved. This is especially important when we are talking about initiating or leading change. People will support the ideas that closely align to the ways they see as "best." Best in this case could simply mean ideas they are comfortable with or have experienced in the past. They aren't best in any objective sense of the word, but best because it's what we prefer. Conversely, ideas that do not support our already held beliefs are viewed as wrong and are harder to implement. On the dissonance side of the ledger, when you try to change a system or tradition in the college, people will often fight your idea simply because it clashes with their strongly held belief on how this should look. The very fact that you want to change it makes some cling to the idea even more strongly.

As a new dean, I attempted to mitigate the effects of confirmation bias and cognitive dissonance in two ways. The first is to assemble a diverse set of advisers to whom you can lean on. For me, this was the Dean's Council. As a leader, we are forced to make decisions. Sometimes these decisions are wrong, and this is normal. In the process of our decision-making, we must try, through talking with people, to make the right choices. The only way to do this as a new dean is to lean on advisers. Of course, having advisers as I am describing takes place from a place of trust.

Leaders must remember that creating genuine trust is not like dumping instant coffee into hot water. A leader who seeks to operate effectively over the long term needs to minimize turnover among his senior advisers in order to allow trust and candor to develop on a solid foundation. (Sample, 2002, p. 25)

Second, talk less and listen more. In Todd Davis' book *Get Better* (2017, pp. 133–134), he discusses the reasons why leaders tend to talk more than they should.

1. *We are trained to talk more.* We are schooled, in the course of becoming leaders, in the art of communicating ideas to others. We aren't attuned as we need to be to the other side of this equation. The listening part. Work on this.
2. *We're fixers by nature.* The deans I have enjoyed working for were people who fixed things. But, sometimes in our efforts to fix, we drown out the thoughts and wishes of others. We just want to help. We can still help, but we should make an effort to listen, first.
3. *The world is in a hurry.* This one is particularly pertinent to my first-year experiences. Some days it seems like everything is coming at you at a million miles an hour. In this setting, our communication tends to mirror our environment. If the environment is fast, our communication with others tends to be fast. Slow down. Better yet, come to a complete stop. And, listen. Just because the world is in a hurry, it doesn't mean that you have to be.
4. *We want to be right.* Of course we do. But in the course of wanting to be right, we engage in selective hearing (remember cognitive dissonance?). Yes. We all do it. Because we want to be right. Let go of this desire, and your ability to listen automatically gets better. Let it go, and listen.

Listening to your people with these things in mind help us to a better picture of the issue in front of us. It sometimes seems that it'd be easier to go solo and make decisions with your gut feelings. This sounds simpler and probably aligns with the archetypical idea of what leadership is supposed to look like. The problem with this is twofold. First, taking on the entire burden of leadership yourself will lead to burnout and undue stress. This job is stressful enough without taking on everything by yourself. The second reason this is problematic is that you are just as susceptible to confirmation bias and cognitive bias as anyone else. You aren't immune. Your advisers and the questions you ask can help you get to the root of problems that you are attempting to solve.

What Would This Look Like If It Were Easy?

The only true voyage would be not to travel
through a hundred different lands with the same pair of eyes,
but to see the same land through a hundred different pairs of eyes.

—Marcel Proust

In Tim Ferris's book *Tribe of Mentors* (2017), he has an idea that I have found to be useful in how I think about the task of helping people solve their problems. Notice that I did not say solve people's problems, but rather helping people to see a path to helping themselves solve issues. The following sentence is one that I used with my faculty and leadership team on a regular basis, and it points to the power of reframing problems and shifting our mindset around problems that confront us. The sentence is "What would this look like if it were easy?" (p. xi). Ferris writes:

> Then, I did what I often do—whether considering a business decision, personal relationship, or otherwise—I asked myself the one question that helps answer many others . . .
>
> What would this look like if it were easy?
>
> "This" could be anything. That morning, it was answering a laundry list of big questions.
>
> "What would this look like if it were easy?" is such a lovely and deceptively leveraged question. It's easy to convince yourself that things need to be hard, that if you're not redlining, you're not trying hard enough. This leads us to look for paths of most resistance, creating unnecessary hardship in the process.
>
> But what happens if we frame things in terms of elegance instead of strain? In doing so, we sometimes find incredible results with ease instead of stress. Sometimes, we "solve" the problem by simply rewording it. (p. xii)

I read this passage right before my time as dean started. When I first read it, I remember being struck at how simple of an idea it was. It is simple because it's about how we orient ourselves to problems. It allows us to see things from a position of possibility and perspective. During my first year as dean, I kept this idea in the front of my mind. I shared this idea with several people when trying to create a new way of doing something or when trying to solve a persistent problem within the college. Some of these people liked the idea and the way that it directed them to simpler answers; some didn't get it and just ignored the idea altogether. This idea works because it helps us get past the idea that the problem before us is too hard or difficult or intractable to resolve. If something is perceived as too difficult to solve, then we usually don't try to solve it. We accept it, and allow it to impact our lives. If our default position is that something is un-solvable, then why try to solve it? But, what if the issue isn't as difficult as we think it is? What if we are wrong about how much work will be necessary to fix something? As we have seen from the research in psychology, human beings are wrong all the time—we just can't see that we are wrong. What if that one thing that keeps you from reaching your potential isn't as hard to fix as you've convinced yourself it is? What if it was easy to fix, instead of hard? What would your actions look like? When you get that picture in your head, you have made the first step. I believe that people do difficult, seemingly impossible things every day because their default position is one of possibility.

This is possible. This is something I can do. Believe it first, then do it.

References

Davis, T. (2017). *Get better: 15 proven practices to build effective relationships at work.* New York, NY: NY: Simon & Schuster.

Ferris, T. (2017). *Tribe of mentors: Short life advice from the best in the world.* Boston, MA: Houghton Mifflin Harcourt.

Holiday, R. (2014). *The obstacle is the way: The timeless art of turning trials into triumph.* New York, NY: Penguin Books.

Plato (1992). *Republic.* (G.M.A. Grube, Trans.). Indianapolis, IN: Hackett.

Radical [Def 1 and 2]. (n.d.). In Oxford Living Dictionary. Retrieved July 1, 2018 from https://en.oxforddictionaries.com/definition/us/radical

Sample, S. (2002). *The contrarian's guide to leadership.* San Francisco, CA: Jossey-Bass.

Thought Monkey. (2017, October 25). *Confirmation bias in 5 minutes* [Video file]. Retrieved from https://www.youtube.com/watch?v=0xKklLplngs

6

Where You Stand Depends on Where You Sit

There are three essentials to leadership: humility, clarity and courage.
—Fuchan Yuan

BIG IDEA FOR THIS CHAPTER

Going from faculty to the deanship is an adjustment on several fronts. The changes in authority, responsibility, and longer hours are the most readily apparent. Another aspect of the dean's office that takes getting used to is the perspective that you must take. Being a professor is, most of the time, a solitary endeavor. You teach your courses, advise your students, conduct research, and publish your work. I have even heard tenured professors give this advice to new people: be selfish, look out for yourself. Being a dean isn't like this. At all. When you are a dean, the decisions that you make impact the entire college. This is a weighty responsibility. It's a responsibility that can pull you in opposite directions. There is a tension between the old you (i.e., pre-dean) and the current you (i.e., leader of the college). This tension can be resolved by reminding yourself of the different role that you now play. You are the caretaker of the college.

"Where You Stand Depends on Where You Sit" is a statement attributed to Rufus Miles, Jr. who was an assistant secretary under Presidents Dwight D. Eisenhower, John F. Kennedy and Lyndon B. Johnson. This maxim is from his 1978 work *The Origin and Meaning of Miles' Law* (as cited in McKinney, 2008). Variously quoted by leaders since then, I came across this idea when reading *Provost: Experiences, Reflections and Advice From a Former "Number Two" on Campus* (Nielsen, 2013). The premise of this statement is a simple one, and it has helped me frame how to view the actions of faculty, staff, and other administrators at my university. Simply put, we make decisions based on where we are within the organization's structure. It's not a judgment on right or wrong, it's more of a descriptor that looks at why. Why we do things depends on where we are. Where we are located within the structure of the organization determines what pressures we feel, what goals we have, and ultimately how we frame an issue or problem. It allows for multiple solutions to a problem to be, in effect, correct. A faculty member can view a problem through the professor lens, develop a solution, and this solution can be appropriate to this problem at this point in time. This is true because it fits the needs and desires of the professor. This same problem viewed through an administrator's lens, with different pressures and goals is likely to have a different solution. Sitting in the dean's chair and sitting in a professor's chair are indeed different. Where we sit frames the stance, and perspective we bring to the table, and this determines were we stand on an issue.

Where We Sit

Staff, faculty, and leadership can be guilty of thinking of problems and issues too narrowly. I know that in my professor role I have looked at issues from the standpoint of how they may or may not impact my teaching, scholarship, and service obligations. If the issue negatively impacts or hinders these areas, I was more likely to have negative views of these issues. For professors, I think that this way of making decisions and determining where you stand on an issue is framing these issues around the ideal existence of a professor. Ideally, these three areas would frame the decisions that professors make. But to do so removes other forces from the equation. These are forces that department chairs and deans must always consider. In my role as chair and now as dean, I have always tried to take as many perspectives into account when making decisions. I have found that the perspective of sitting in the dean's chair is not only different from that of the chair and of faculty and staff, but that it requires, more than any role I have had, an eye toward the future. It's a look at not only what is good for today, but what is good for the college in three to five years from now. In the case of hiring faculty or other personnel actions, my decisions have much bigger consequences. I think these decisions can be a hard sell for many because they aren't used to taking the long view of problems and their solutions. As dean, I sit in the dean's chair; the dean's chair is at the intersection of past and future, faculty and administration, old and new.

When I was a faculty member, my concerns were mostly selfish and linear. I knew what I wanted and I knew how they impacted my teaching, scholarship, and service. Because these are the parts of my job that determined whether or not I earned tenure, this made sense (see Hendrickson, Lane, Harris, & Dorman, 2013 discussion on collective individualism). As a dean, my concerns are mostly outward facing and non-linear. If concerns and decision making as a professor can be represented by a line, the concerns and decision making process as a dean can be represented by a web—everything and every decision is connected to something else. Move one part, and a ripple effect is felt throughout the system.

Budget

Making decisions about the budget are probably the hardest because you have more knowledge and insight about what money you have and where it can be spent. Many times, faculty see these decisions in individual terms, and fail to see how their requests are tied to the larger budget outlook. During my first year, it was helpful to discuss the budget with the leadership team and at times with the entire faculty. This was a version of transparency that allowed faculty to see that their request for money was tied to larger concerns. I say that this was a "version" of transparency because it was not total transparency. It was my attempt to help them understand why I made certain decisions, not so they had full access to all of the budget lines. The structure of budgets in colleges can take many forms, from highly regulated, top down models where your revenue streams are varied, to models that are centered on the dean and decisions at the college level. The budget I worked with during my first year as dean closely resembled the first model. One of our revenue sources was the accumulation of a fee that we placed on upper division hours within one of our departments. Historically, the college used this money to support teacher education students and faculty travel related to certain topics. When I first started, there were many questions about how much money was in this particular account, how the money was allotted, and how faculty could use these funds. In the name of transparency, I showed the faculty this information—how much money we took in each year, how it is used, and how much we could use to support students and faculty. This was a departure from the previous years in that the actual numbers were being discussed in an open meeting. Although there weren't any shocking revelations about the money nor was there a large amount that was "left over" to spend, faculty appreciated being in the loop about this fund.

Enrollment

In my experiences, faculty generally don't see increases in enrollment as a pressing matter. They are concerned with teaching their classes, conducting research and writing, and keeping up with their service commitments on campus and in their respective fields. Upper administrators, particularly provosts and presidents, on the other hand, see enrollment as a major part of their responsibilities as university leaders. Deans, not surprisingly, are caught in the middle. As a dean, I am forced to see all sides of this issue. As a professor I preferred smaller class sizes to larger ones. As a dean, I am charged with making sure that budgetary concerns are a primary factory in making decisions about enrollment, especially class sizes. Again, this isn't a concern that I had as a professor, but as a dean it is a semester-by-semester issue. Most colleges and departments have class enrollment guidelines that can guide these decisions, and it helped me to have these conversations with my department chairs early on in the course scheduling process. In this case, clarity around the guidelines early in this process allows you to be proactive in how we close or combine sections of courses.

Political Capital

During your first year as dean, you will notice that people begin to ascribe power and authority to you that you don't actually have. Remember that deans are middle managers; we manage and lead from the middle. We are situated between the faculty and upper administration. In this case, "where you sit" determines how people view your influence and "pull" with the people a level above you in the organizational chart. Sometimes this realization from others is subtle and sometimes it's not so subtle. This takes some getting used to as a new dean. People begin to talk to you about different issues with a different tone of voice. How you respond to issues and problems within the college cannot be narrowly focused like when you were a faculty member.

Your frame of reference shifts from your own personal preferences and concerns to the concerns of the entire college. This fact is due to the symbolic power that you now possess. Notice that I say symbolic power in this case. This is important because the office you hold is one where political power is situational. You don't actually have as much power as people think you do, so be careful with how you speak, act, and make decisions (Jenkins, 2018). It should be noted that this isn't a face we show faculty in order to hide our true intentions on issues. This isn't a political ploy to hide how much power we really have. It's simply the default position that we need to have. Broadly look at issues and make decisions for the good of the entire college.

Accreditation

The process of earning accreditation from your state or professional organization is a laborious, time-consuming process. It also represents one of the best examples of the "where you stand depends on where you sit" rule. Faculty concerned with teaching and research view accreditation efforts as a task that takes away from the important parts of their job. Having worked in several colleges of education, I have yet to meet the faculty member who is overly excited to work on state or national accreditation. I think part of this attitude rests with the bureaucracy that is a part of state and national organizations charged with guiding these processes. Another part of this rests with our failure of leaders/deans to frame accreditation in its proper place. Accreditation should not be thought of as one more committee to serve on. Accreditation should involve the improvement of all that you do within a college or university. It should be interwoven into the way that you develop programs and how those programs are offered. The goal of accreditation is continuous improvement and quality programs, but for faculty this message is sometimes lost in the myriad of other tasks they must tend to. For faculty, accreditation is often viewed as a type of service to the college, and this is technically true. It's just much bigger than that. It's the assurance that we are doing the things we need to do to maintain our status and standing in the academic community.

New Programs

Deans are required to manage people and resources. They do this with the people above their administrative level (president, provost, vice provost, etc.) and they do this with people below their administrative level (department chairs, directors, associate deans, program coordinators, staff, etc.). Much of what a dean does in his day-to-day work life involves managing from the middle, navigating these two worlds to accomplish goals for the college.

Just because something is a good idea, doesn't mean that we should do it. In keeping with the "where you sit" idea, new programs are conceived and developed at the provost level, usually as a way to boost enrollment or at the departmental level. There is a current tendency to build programs because someone has a good idea. As a new dean, you will feel these pressures to develop new programs, to innovate existing programs, or as the tired expression goes, to think outside the box. I think that this idea deserves more caution. We should only develop new programs if there is a clear market and need for these programs. This, of course, is common sense. In the rush to create new programs to boost enrollment or to outdo other universities, we get caught in a cycle of creating simply to create. Just because something is a good idea, doesn't mean that we should do it. As a dean the pressure to approve of or give the green light to projects is a major part of the job. In my experience, this part of your job involves saying no to projects that do not have a viable long-term outlook or projection. In fact, colleges sometimes develop new programs or offerings to fit a niche (sometimes in the form of a certificate) only to have the fad pass in a couple years. Sometimes this niche is in response to the market or in the case of colleges of education, in response to local school district needs. Another part of this dilemma is the creative capacity of your college when it comes to creating new programs. Larger colleges, with more faculty, staff, and support resources are better able to engage in this activity. Thinking of program development with the line from the movie Field of Dreams "If we build it, they will come," seems to be the strategy of some colleges. This position on program development is feasible inasmuch as your resources allow for it. The larger your faculty and staff and the more resources you bring to bear on this task, the easier your people will have it. Having worked at small universities and large universities, I can comfortably say that smaller colleges should refrain from getting caught in the cycle of creating a program, experiencing a short-term boost, followed by declining enrollment.

Explaining Changes (Over and Over)

As you are moving between the levels of your college and university, it is imperative that you maintain a steady stream of communication with the people below you and above you. This was something that I learned as a department chair that I have realized is even more important as a dean. This idea is simply noticing the importance of a steady, consistent message to your people. This is especially important in times of change, and as a new dean, there was plenty of change. There was change not simply because the college had a new dean. There were new programs, new state regulations, and new faculty in new positions. Managing change is a daily consideration from the dean's chair. With this in mind, we should make an effort to explain why we have made decisions. We should be ready to explain these changes and their rationale to different groups, over and over. The reason for this is simple, and its something that I think we all know, intuitively, is true. New information or a change in our work environment doesn't always stick in people's minds. As a new dean, you aren't really sure why new things aren't taking hold immediately, you just know that people act as if they don't know what you are talking about—even though you have talked about this multiple times. In some cases, they may not remember because they are having a hard time managing the volume of change. Maybe the old way of doing things is so ingrained in the operations of the college that they revert back to the old way out of habit. Or maybe they think that your new way of doing something won't really stick for the long haul and they are going to wait it out, hoping that the college will return to the old ways of doing something.

All or none of these may be operating; I think the most common explanation for this phenomenon is that humans just don't listen carefully or remember new information well. I know that I am guilty of this. I am reminded of this when I give directions to a group of people. Even with my most organized and well thought out plans, there are still a good number of people who don't understand what I am asking them to do, or who need the information/directions repeated. I have seen this with the middle school children I used to teach, and I see it with adults as well. Constant, consistent messaging not only helps your people understand what changes have been made and why, it also helps you, as the dean, think through your decisions. I have found that the more I have to explain a change or innovation that we have made, the logic and rationale for the decision becomes clearer to me as well. Sometimes in the process of explaining a change, I realize that there are better ways to explain the very thing I am trying to explain. It becomes a meta-explanation. It's as though I am exercising my explanation skills. The more I do it, the better I become at it. If we have changes that we make, and these changes are important to the operation of the college and help us meet our goals of excellent teaching, scholarship, and service, be ready to repeat yourself. Constant consistent messaging.

Help Your Leadership Team to Think Like a Dean

Initiating and creating change within your college takes more than your good ideas. Sure, there may be occasions in which your idea and your thinking about an issue drives change in your organization. But as my first year shows, change is just about the only constant that I had as a first year dean.

You can't, nor should you, manage all change by yourself. Previously, I discussed the idea of a Dean's Council and how it helped me think through, make, and implement change my first year. During our meetings as a council we really had two kinds of meetings. First, we had meetings where a college specific topic or issue was discussed. In these meetings, the department chairs, the associate dean, the director of teacher education, and my senior staff did most of the talking. Since they know how things were done in the past, they were well positioned to help me see problems from different perspectives. In this first type of meeting, I would propose a sketch of a solution and let the conversation unfold. I called these meetings "problem solving meetings." A second type of meeting that we had for our council my first year is what I would call "developmental meetings." The focus and point of these meetings was less about solving a specific problem and more about helping the team to think about being better thinkers and problem solvers. If the first type of meeting was getting an answer, the second type was helping people to be better leaders. I shared some examples of what we did in our meetings that fall into this category. I was attempting to help the team see that there are different ways to think about problem solving, learn about leadership, and to become better, more thoughtful leaders. One way to do this is through the use of case studies.

Case studies are not new to leadership studies or degree programs in leadership. When I participated in the Management Development Program at Harvard, much of the curriculum that we used was in the form of case studies. Two books that I used during my first year were *Higher Education Administration* (2015) by Scott Newman and *A Toolkit for Deans* by Patricia Mosto and Dianne Dorland (2014). Mosto and Dorland write:

> . . . we find case studies and scenarios useful. They have served as learning tools for seeing how others have solved problems and help us think about how we will solve our own. We also found it useful to think about problems or issues beforehand and hear how other deans handled situations, even if our eventual choices were different. (p. x)

In addition to using case studies and scenarios with your team as a way to build leadership capacity, exercises like these allow your team to see the "where you sit" idea more clearly. Most of my leadership team had not been in other levels of leadership in the university level. Working our way through real problems (in our job) and fictional problems (via case studies) drives home the point that perspective matters and that our positions within the college frame how we see, respond to, and eventually solve problems. An additional perk of doing this sort of work with your team is that it helps them to think more like a dean. Some clarification is needed on that last sentence. I am not saying that any of the team desires to be a dean or that they are planning to become a dean, but rather, I am helping them to think like a dean (at least part of the time). Imagine what your leadership team would sound like and what their work would look like, if they took the time to learn about the perspectives of the other parts of the college. This isn't to say that everyone would understand every part of everyone else's role. That's a knowledge issue (i.e., knowing everything about another subunit). I am speaking to the idea of perspective. It requires knowing something about the other subunits and taking different perspective on the work that's being done in that area. This perspective requires a serious effort to understand the pressures, constraints, and dilemmas inherent in someone else's world. Case studies help with this.

It is also helpful as a leader to remember that we operate between "the reality of human nature, as opposed to what [we] wished it were" (Sample, 2002, p. 102). There is a delicate balance between seeing the good in people's motives and taking on a perspective that assumes the worst in people. I tend to default to the former idea, sometimes to my detriment. I have met other leaders who take as their default position that people will always succumb to their lesser angels in participating in the life of your college, that they will always behave in self-serving and underhanded ways. I think that people who have a steadfast and rigid default position here make a mistake. I would include myself in this group. I often make the mistake of thinking of this in binary terms, when this idea is much more complicated and nuanced. There were times during the first year as dean where I was burned by a faculty member or in a decision I made because I naively assumed that they were being honest and had the college's best interests at heart. I mistakenly assumed that because I saw the college a certain way (globally, from the dean's office), that they did too (they didn't). There were times when people told me things that were falsehoods, easily proven, that didn't serve the faculty member, the leadership team, the college, or the new dean. Days like these were particularly difficult because they reveal something about our faculty and perhaps ourselves that we often forget. We sometimes do things we shouldn't do to gain the upper hand in a situation. My advice for new deans in this area is that you should trust people, but verify what they tell you. This isn't a new idea. And this isn't an oxymoron. I am not saying "trust, but don't trust." I am saying to let your default position be that you trust people in your college, but also recognize that your trust in people can be a liability in the information you receive—information that you will use to make future decisions. Verifying what you are told does two things for you as a new dean. It allows you to check your understanding of a situation against what you were told to see if you are seeing the situation correctly, and it allows you to determine if you were given false information. Verifying information leads to a better understanding of the issue. If the information you use to make future decisions is not accurate, that leaves you open to attack. "The challenge of the leader isn't to delude himself into thinking that people are intrinsically better or worse than they really are; it is to find ways to bring out the best in his followers (and in himself) while minimizing the worst" (Sample, 2002, p. 105). Trust, but verify.

Remembering What it Was Like Being a Faculty Member

Perhaps this idea—where you sit—is as simple as taking other people's perspective into account when making decisions. Or at the very least acknowledging how others see an issue or problem. Keep in mind, this isn't about deciding who is right or who has the best idea (although that matters too), but rather that we notice how one's position determines the filter through which ideas are viewed. Below I list five issues that a dean faces on a regular basis. For experienced deans, I am sure that these issues are dealt with in a routine fashion. For new deans, they are probably dispatched with in a less than routine way—and that's okay. Step one is to make sure that you are taking a broad view of how others see the issue. Again, just because a group sees an issue in a particular way, that doesn't mean you will agree with them. But attempting to understand how others see the issue will help you make a more informed decision and it will help you to explain your rationale to people after the decision is made. In that way, "where you sit" is an explanatory tool for decision-making. It serves as a frame through which decisions are made and how they are explained to people who are impacted. Below, let's look at class size, hiring, new program development, budget, scheduling, and change. The examples I provide below are not exhaustive, nor are they intended to represent all faculty, deans, and upper administrators. They are intended to be illustrative of the types of divergent thinking that these groups have on any one issue. This sort of exercise helped me in my first year to shift from diverse and divergent thinking to more convergent thinking when it came to making decisions. The exercise below helps new deans to see how they are managing from the middle and the pressures that this includes. This idea developed into an exercise that I did whenever I was trying to think through a problem. It's simple: get a sheet of paper, divide it into three sections, and sketch out how (you think) faculty see an issue, how you see the issue, and how (you think) the provost sees the issue. A note of caution: this exercise involves you thinking about what you think people think about an issue. Yes. That's a confusing sentence. Again: this exercise involves you thinking about what you think people think about an issue. This sort of exercise is a starting point for your thinking about issues. But, it never hurts to actually ask the people you work with what their thoughts are on a topic. When all else fails, just ask.

Issue 1: Class Size

Faculty

Faculty that I have worked with almost always want lower class sizes. This is not brand-new information. When I was a faculty member I preferred to teach courses that had 15–20 students over courses with 40–50 students. I found that the course was easier to manage, I was able to form stronger relationships with students, and there was less grading. There is research on smaller class sizes being better for all involved—students and instructors. The overall experience of the course was better. I have worked in departments where there was an expectation that courses of 30 or more students be divided into two sections instead of one. In this way, instructors would have smaller sections of the same course prep.

Dean

As a dean you were probably a professor before you took on the role of leader of the college. If this is the case, you are familiar with the previous discussion. As dean you are aware of the rationale behind smaller class sizes. As dean you have a responsibility to ensure that the needs of students are met, that faculty have a fair teaching workload, and that the college is getting its money's worth when it comes to the amount of students who are taught by full time faculty. That last sentence (and the thinking behind it) was never a consideration when I was a faculty member. As dean, it is one of the primary considerations. During my first year as dean, I compiled a list of full time and part time instructors that included the number of courses they were teaching and the total number of students. The exercise itself is not intended to determine who has a quality course or who is (or isn't) working hard. But it does give you an overall picture of who is teaching your college's students. It may also tip you off to a trend that I believe we should change. Do your part-time or adjunct faculty teach more of your students than your full-time faculty? If so, this is an opportunity to ascertain why the lowest paid people in the college are shouldering the majority of the teaching load.

Provost

The provosts that I have worked for wanted deans to make sure that full time faculty were teaching full loads whenever possible. And, by whenever possible, I mean always. In looking at how many students that faculty are teaching, provosts can, in a sense, examine the health of a college. A full time faculty member who teaches four courses with a combined total of 17 students paints a negative picture for the provosts I have worked with. If you have a full time faculty member teaching 17 students, and temporary faculty member teaching 100 students, provosts are right to ask if we are utilizing our resources effectively. In this case, provosts typically view this idea from the macro level: number of sections of courses, total students, total number of majors, and credit hour production.

Issue 2: Hiring

Faculty

When a faculty member retires or leaves the institution for another opportunity, there is a chance to fill the existing faculty line with a new person. This can be an exciting time for the faculty and chair in that department because they have an opportunity to seek out and find a talented person to join their team. Typically the chair and the department are looking to replace what was lost. This, on the surface, makes a lot of sense. Thinking about the replacement considers the outgoing person's service obligations, teaching responsibilities, and area of expertise. The logic is as follows—We have lost the professor that taught educational assessment, so we need to hire someone to teach assessment. In thinking of hiring in this way, we are replacing one person for another; the person we hire is expected to fit into the spot that is now vacant.

Dean

As a dean, you have no doubt served or chaired numerous search committees. If you have served in these roles, you know that faculty tend to look for one-to-one replacements for the people who have left the university. Even as the dean, your interests in who to hire are also tied up in the concerns that the chair and the department have. Since you must consider the needs of the entire college, your concerns should be broader in scope. The question that I asked myself was: "Are there other college needs that a new person could help us with?" I think of this as running faculty searches with overall college needs in mind. This can be accomplished by meeting with your leadership team and discussing the needs of the college. How do we recruit someone that can teach specific classes, but who also possesses a particular (needed) skill set? Taking the prior example as a case in point, we needed someone to replace the faculty who taught educational assessment. Writing a job advertisement for the person to teach this class is pretty straightforward. The college also needed someone to serve as the "Assessment Coordinator" for our accreditation efforts. So, we decided to write the job advertisement to include teaching responsibilities and skills that would be required of a college assessment coordinator. The job advertisement made this explicit to interested candidates. The expectations of this job are to teach certain classes and to serve the college as in other ways. In this way our advertisements are specific and targeted to the people that we need.

Provost

The provosts I have worked for didn't get into the specifics of what a job advertisement should look like. They left these discussions and decisions to department chairs and deans. They have typically signed off on job advertisements to replace lost faculty and in some cases to approve new lines for my college. The area where the provost and the dean levels will cross is in cases where you will ask the provost for additional resources to perform a part of the college's function. For example, you and your college are preparing for your accreditation cycle. You may notice that you need an outside consultant or someone to assist with your data collection and/or interpretation. Provosts predictably ask you if you have current faculty who can assist with these tasks. If you have current faculty on staff that can perform these tasks, the provost is less likely to give you additional resources. This is where being creative with your job advertisements can help you as a first year dean. Think about the big picture when hiring your faculty, and hire people who can help with actually running the college, as opposed to just teaching and research. In an era of decreasing state and federal resources flowing to universities, this will ensure that you have the right people in the right positions to run the college. This idea was always in the forefront of my mind during my first year. During my first year as dean, we conducted five faculty searches, and had one person retire. Although it is too early to tell what impact these decisions will have, I believe that one of the most important legacies that deans can have is in the people they hire.

Issue 3: New Program Development

Faculty

As faculty, new program development can be a lot of work. In colleges of education, new program development is often in response to a state mandate or need of the public schools. The processes and guidelines usually required for a new program constitute a laborious process of paperwork from the state department of education and possibly your regional/national accreditor. Even with these constraints in mind, faculty often want to create new programs in your college. Sometimes faculty want to create new degree programs (at the undergraduate or graduate levels), professional certificates (12–15 hours), or adjustments to existing offerings. On one end of the spectrum you have faculty who want to create new programs because it fits their particular research niche or field of expertise. On the other end, you have new program development because the state has mandated these changes. In a resource poor environment, the former example is a bad idea; the latter is a requirement. There may even be cases in which new programs are put forth by the faculty because you are the new dean. Perhaps this program was denied or delayed under a previous administration, and faculty are trying to see if they can get it approved under new leadership. In these cases, it is useful to determine why it was not created before you arrived. Ask lots of questions.

Dean

When it comes to new program development, you are interested in broader concerns than are faculty. The central questions for deciding on new programs are: (a) Does this serve our student population? (b) Is this something that the state has mandated or is it optional? (c) Do we have the resources/faculty to develop this new program? and (d) What are the unintended consequences of this new program? These questions are probably best considered by you in conjunction with your leadership team. Program development and maintenance are expensive endeavors and with decreasing budgets, increased accountability, and higher standards, new programs are to be pursued with caution. As the dean, you have to determine if these new ideas for program development are actually needed by the college, or it they represent a passing fad or interest. For deans in colleges of education, the focus of your inquiry should be student, state, and resource oriented. If it meets these three tests, then the idea is probably one you should pursue. If the new program idea does not serve the student, meet a new state requirement, and drains existing resources, you should redirect your faculty to other development projects. Not every idea that faculty have for a new program is something that you should pursue. This doesn't mean that their idea is a bad idea. But, there are external forces that constrain what we can do in the area of program creation and development.

Provost

Provosts are almost always interested in higher enrollment for the university. I have worked for five provosts and each one made enrollment one of the highest priorities of their job. I have heard several of these provosts say, "The quickest way to higher enrollment is to create new programs." This is probably true, but can represent a shortsighted goal for the college. Creating programs to boost enrollment serves to put faculty in a position of creating programs (which is a lot of work) for a short-term gain. The other consideration from the provost's office (and by default, your office) comes in the form of resources. If there is a push from the provost to create new programs, does this mean that your college will receive additional resources to make and maintain these changes? For example, will your college get additional faculty lines to implement these new programs or will you have to use existing resources/faculty lines? Will you receive additional funds in the budget to create this new program, or will you have to use existing monies to carry out this plan? As the dean, your responsibility to your college is to ensure that the work being done in these cases serves the long-term needs of the college and that resources are available.

Issue 4: Budget

Faculty

Every position I have held in higher education, there was a perception that the leader (dean, provost, president) had more money in the budget than they were willing to admit. Whether or not this is true is another story, but that was the perception. The people that I worked with were fairly certain that the dean of the college was somehow withholding the real value of the budget from faculty. People have told me that I have large sums of money at my disposal. They are certain that the former dean was sitting on large cash accounts from which I could give them—if I wanted to. When I talk to the people who run the budgets for the university and I look at my college budgets, I come to a conclusion pretty quickly. This money does not exist. This perception is created when you aren't transparent with the big picture. Notice that I say big picture. I believe that your faculty should know, generally, how budgets are organized in your college. They don't have to know how much you decide to spend on necessary expenditures or how these budgets are allocated, but a general idea of the budget helps. Secrecy breeds conspiracy theories. Faculty tend to view budgets in much the same way that they view new programs. They view it with their interests in mind, without having to consider larger implications. They want what they want, and they believe they should get it. If faculty don't have a general idea of the types of budgets in the college, they will assume that you are denying their requests out of a personal decision that you are making. If they have this knowledge, they will know that you are making a budgetary decision, not a personal one.

Dean

As dean, your role is to ensure that the resources of your college are being used to support the core functions of teaching, research, service, and outreach. In my previous jobs in higher education, I was not completely responsible for the budget. I was typically the approver, at some level, of what money was being spent. In the dean's role, the entire college budget falls to you. Oftentimes, the decisions that I made my first year revolved around what people wanted versus what the college needed. Once the needs were taken care of, then we could look more closely at what people wanted. At my regular meetings with the provost, the budget was a consistent topic of discussion. This was due to the fact that we were starting several new programs and hiring new faculty. Since I was new to both of these processes from the dean's chair, there was a learning curve for me in these areas. Another aspect of this learning curve that should be noted: each college that I have worked in has conducted budgeting and finances differently. The concepts and terms are largely the same, but the processes for requesting and spending funds, making requests for funding, etc. were all specific to the college where I worked. Overall though, the stance I took as a dean was different from my other roles in that I had to concern myself with the entire college, not just a department or program. Going from specific to global, small picture to big picture was an adjustment. My starting point was always—does this serve the mission of our college? This idea guided my decision making my first year.

Provost

The provost is forced to see the budget from an even larger perspective. I think of this in concentric circles with the smaller circles in the center representing faculty and their narrow interests, larger with the dean and college concerns, and largest with the Provost and the entire academic operation of the university. For most provosts, their decisions are informed by two sources, the president of the university and the university's strategic plan. This has been the standard operating procedure at the universities where I have worked. A new experience for me was making public requests for resources/funds to the provost for the next academic year. In this process, college deans (in collaboration with their department chairs and faculty), developed requests that were to be considered by the provost and central administration. These requests were largely situated around program needs, recruitment, and innovative aspects of our college. Most importantly, these requests were related to the goals of the president and the university's strategic plan documents. The idea was clear: ideas that were aligned with and in support of the university's long range plan were more likely to get approved and funded.

Issue 5: Scheduling

Faculty

Sometimes faculty can view the scheduling of courses through their own needs and desires. Unless you have ever created a schedule, you are probably unaware of the many moving parts that go into this task. In colleges of education this is especially complicated. You have core courses from arts and sciences, a professional core of education courses, and of course, field experiences and internships. Faculty who have taught the same courses for many years, in the same time slot, in the same classroom are particularly susceptible to narrow thinking on this topic. It isn't that they are being selfish about when their courses are offered, but this is more the result of not realizing how complicated scheduling courses for a department or college can be. Because faculty are concerned with their classes and their classes alone, they cannot see the big picture of why certain courses are offered at certain times.

Dean

Deans, once again, are put in the position of having to see the big picture. I am more than willing to give faculty their choice of courses, in the time slot that they desire, as long as it serves the needs of the student, the program, and the department. These considerations also include the delivery mode or the time of day that courses are offered. For example, we have a program in our college that is oriented towards working professionals in the schools. It is designed for people who have an associate's degree and currently work as aides or teaching assistants in schools. Given these people's work schedules, we have decided to offer more of these courses in the evening to accommodate their work situations.

Provost

Provosts are likely to view this through two lenses: budget and enrollment. From the budgetary lens, provosts want to ensure that we are getting our money's worth when it comes to when courses are offered and how this impacts a professor's credit hour production. A provost is likely to see this in terms of how many students or credit hours a professor is teaching during a certain semester. The best example here is the professor who teaches two small sections of a course when he could teach one large section. Teaching the one large section would free this professor to teach another section of something else, oftentimes instead of hiring a part time instructor to teach the second course. On the other hand, I have worked with provosts who see scheduling as a way to boost enrollment for the university overall. In this line of thinking, colleges should offer as many classes as possible in as many formats to ensure that potential students have options when making their college selection.

The examples listed above all deal with managing change. As a dean, especially a new dean, this is a central part of the job. This involves collecting information about the situation, looking at the big picture, recognizing that your decisions are based on the position you have and the roles that you play (i.e., where you sit), and having the courage to make tough decisions. These decisions and the way you manage them are about change. I want to conclude this chapter with a list of tips from Buller's (2007) *The Essential Academic Dean: A Practical Guide to College Leadership.* I reflected on this list (and Buller's recommendations) often during my first year as dean. This list helped remind me that...

1. Whenever possible, see a consensus recommendation on the need for reform from an established and respected group (p. 44).
2. Try to identify alternative solutions to the problem before embarking on a plan (p. 45).
3. Consider exploring all feasible alternatives with focus groups (p. 46).
4. If at all possible, create a cost-benefit analysis for the reform you are considering (p. 46).
5. Communicate as extensively as possible about plans for reform as they develop (p. 47).
6. Understand that men and women may respond differently to reform and may even approach the process of change differently (p. 47).

References

Buller, J. (2007). *The essential academic dean: A practical guide to college leadership.* San Francisco, CA: Jossey-Bass.

Hendrickson, R., Lane, J., Harris, J., & Dorman, R. (2013). *Academic leadership and governance of higher education: A guide for trustees, leaders, and aspiring leaders of two- and four-year institutions.* Sterling, VA: Stylus.

Jenkins, R. (2018, July 5). Do you really want to be a dean? *ChronicleVitae* Retrieved from https://chroniclevitae.com/news/2076-do-you-really-want-to-be-a-dean

McKinney, M. (2018, February 25). *Miles' Law and six other maxims of management.* [Blog post]. Retrieved from https://www.leadershipnow.com/leadingblog/2008/02/miles_law_and_six_other_maxims.html

Mosto, P., & Dorland, D. (2014). *A toolkit for deans.* Lanham, MD: Rowman & Littlefield.

Newman, S. (2015). *Higher education administration: 50 case-based vignettes.* Charlotte, NC: Information Age.

Nielsen, L. (2013). *Provost: Experiences, reflections and advice from a former "number two" on campus.* New York, NY: Stylus.

Sample, S. (2002). *The contrarian's guide to leadership.* San Francisco, CA: Jossey-Bass.

7

Take Care of Yourself

*If you look into your own heart, and you find nothing wrong there,
what is there to worry about? What is there to fear?*

—Confucius

BIG IDEA FOR THIS CHAPTER

BIG IDEA

Leadership at the dean's level can be an exhausting and trying experience. The first year is particularly daunting because you are required to make decisions with partial information and because you are, well, new. In a sense, everything is new. Having to navigate a world in which everything is new requires a lot of mental and physical effort. Solid advice that I received from other deans and from my reading is that you should take care of yourself. I have found that most of the ideas for self-care are small changes that we make to our daily routines. The other thing that helps is being able to set expectations for yourself and the people you work with. It's these small changes that make all the difference. I end this chapter with some thoughts on being ethical as a leader.

As a new dean, I found that several things were immediately clear. There would be more demands on my time and that the nature of my work had changed. We get so used to doing the same kind of work (i.e., teaching, researching, advising) that we forget that there are other types of work. As I am sure you already know, the deanship is very different from being a faculty member. Although this may sound like common sense, until you experience it, you can't really understand it. The shifts are pretty drastic. You move to a position of more authority and decision-making power. Your field of concerns grows a hundredfold. You seem to always be on the clock and public facing. Things that you say are interpreted as more than you intended. Decisions that you make are always analyzed and scrutinized. People assign motive to your words and actions that are not always accurate. These experiences—more power, less privacy, always on, and under a microscope—can take a toll. If you have made it to the dean's chair, then you have had taxing leadership roles before. You have no doubt heard deans you have worked for tell you about this aspect of the job. But hearing about the job, and doing the job, are different experiences. The average deanship in colleges of education lasts 4.5 years (Robbins & Schmitt, 1994). This is due, in part, to the many pressures (see Henk, Wepner, Lovell, & Melnick, 2017) that deans face on a daily basis. My first year had its up and downs, and I found the advice that I got from current and former deans to be pretty sound. This job was as difficult as most said it would be. In this chapter I share my thoughts on coping with the demands of being a first-year dean. Some of these deal with self-care, others deal with routines, and others deal with maintaining a semblance of normal life during this job. I dealt with the stresses of the deanship by maintaining daily routines, setting aside time to be screen-free, and setting expectations for myself and my faculty.

The Power of (Morning) Routines

> *The first hour of the morning, is the rudder of the day.*
> —Henry Ward Beecher

I have always been a routines person. When I became a teacher and then a professor, my leadership roles forced this idea upon me. The logic is simple. When your day or the task that you have to accomplish are overwhelming or seem impossible, it's a good idea to put part of your day on autopilot. This is the idea of being proactive. When parts of your day are not on autopilot, you are placed in a situation in which you are constantly responding to your environment. Being reactive is more exhausting than being proactive. Many times, proactive behaviors as a leader take the form of routines, protocols, and processes.

When I became a dean, it seemed as though the day had been compressed. There were so many demands on my time it seemed that the day was simultaneously longer and shorter—longer—because the workday included more hours, but shorter because it didn't seem that I could fit everything in. Not surprisingly, dean time is more structured than faculty time. Outside of teaching courses at designated times and routine meetings in the college, my time was controlled by me and remained largely unstructured. As dean, my time was still owned by me, but there were many more demands on that time. Besides the time that I set aside to be unstructured (that sounds counterintuitive), my days were more structured. I used my unstructured time in the morning and the evening to better support the hectic schedule of being a dean. This was something I had always done in my career, even as a middle school teacher and later when I became faculty at a university. But during my first year as dean, this routine was essential to my work and existence as a dean (and husband and father). It allowed me to compartmentalize parts of my day that would support me during the work portion of the day. My morning routine (Spall & Xander, 2018) was as follows:

4:00 a.m.   *Wake Up (and coffee)*

For those of you who aren't morning people, this one may seem a bit extreme. When most people learn that I start my day at 4:00 a.m., I get comments about how early this is and how they "like to sleep." I also like to sleep. I haven't always gotten up this early in my career. My usual hour to wake up has been 5:30–6:00 a.m., so the change isn't that drastic. Waking up this early allows me adequate time to do the things I need to accomplish before the day begins.

4:05–5:00 a.m.   *Write*

For the first 45–55 minutes of the day, I sit down in my home office and I write. This habit is something that I would recommend for faculty as well as people in leadership. Writing well is a skill that you can improve. With daily practice you become a better writer and thinker. For me, it is helpful to have a designated part of the day to work on articles, book chapters, conference presentations, etc. that I have in the works. It allows me to maintain a connection to scholarship in the field of education. Although I use this time in the morning to work on scholarship, you could use this time to write about your day in review (yesterday), to plan for the day ahead, or to do short and long-range planning. For me, the point isn't what you decide to write about, but rather that you designate a time to sit, think, and write. Some mornings the words flow and you will write a lot; other days, the words will be hard to come by and you will write very little. The purpose is not word count, but the routine and daily practice.

5:00–5:15 a.m.   Meditate

Again, this one strikes many people as odd. I thought it was too. Until I tried it. The mind of a dean is so busy and pulled in many directions that it helps to be able to filter out the noise and focus. Although meditation does not cancel out all noise and distractions, it does help me to focus and to remind me of what matters. I learned about mindfulness meditation at an education conference that I attended. I went to a session out of curiosity that had the words "mindfulness" in the title. During the session, the speaker guided the participants through a basic mindfulness meditation exercise, and I was hooked. After the session I talked with others in attendance and someone mentioned an app for iPhone called "Headspace." That was over 2 years ago, and mindfulness meditation (see Kabat-Zinn, 2005) has been a part of my daily routine ever since. The app (and others like "Calm") guides you through meditation exercises, and gives you tips on how to integrate parts of this practice into your day-to-day interactions with the world. The premise of this practice is simple. By taking the time to practice being mindful, we can be more focused, attentive, and present with our work and the ones we love.

5:30–6:00 a.m.   Run/Exercise

The science is in on this one, so there's no need to go into a ton of explanation on this idea. Since I was in high school, I have been a runner. Not a marathon runner, but more of a 5K–10K type of runner. I have incorporated this into my day since I became a teacher. For me, exercising daily, usually in the form of a 15–20 minute run, is essential to my emotional and physical well-being. If I skip running for a couple days in a row, I am simply not myself. The point here is clear. Daily exercise is a requirement for me if I am to be my best. Not four hours in the gym or running a daily marathon, but a small to moderate amount of exercise every day.

6:00–6:30 a.m.   Breakfast

I cook myself a worthy breakfast every morning. This one is going to depend on your penchant for breakfast foods, so I will leave the menu to the reader, but eating well is key to your performance at work. The act of taking the time to make yourself a real breakfast, instead of grabbing a granola bar on the way out, is a great way to start the day.

6:45–7:10 a.m.   Getting Ready for Work

After breakfast, I take a shower and get dressed for work. I also have a son in school, so part of my morning is situated around making breakfast, getting him dressed, and off to school—all of which are aided by the fact that I do most of my routines before he wakes up.

For readers who are not used to a morning routine, the description of my mornings may seem a bit overkill. The waking up at 4:00 a.m. or the meditation piece or maybe you aren't into exercising (especially at 5:30 in the morning). Here is my advice for you: create routines that work for you and that help you to have a productive and meaningful morning before your workday begins. Are there things you'd like to do that you don't have time for during the day? If so, this is the beginning of your thinking around your routines. Another idea for people who've never tried this is to start small and to take a gradual approach. If you've never gotten up at 4:00 a.m. and if you aren't someone who engages in regular exercise, then you shouldn't probably try to do all of this at the same time. Before becoming dean, I was not used to getting up this early, so I gradually began to wake up 5–10 minutes earlier each day until I reached the desired waking time. The same approach can apply to exercise, writing, or anything else you want to do during your morning routine. Start small, make these activities a habit, and you will have a greater chance of sticking with your plan.

I also have a routine for the evening, but it isn't as involved. Since I have a family and the responsibilities which come with that, my evenings are more unstructured than my mornings. The point of my evening routines is to set the stage for the morning, to ensure that there is a seamless transition from waking in the morning to getting to my routine tasks before I go to work. This many sound silly to include in a book on being a new dean, but I cannot stress how much routines help me to manage the rest of my day (see Anderberg, 2017; *Art of Manliness,* 2015). My evening routine is as follows:

Clothes Ready

I ensure that the next day's clothes have been chosen and are ready to go in my closet. This prevents me from having to make wardrobe decisions in the morning. This is one of the best parts of my routine because it simplifies my morning. One less decision to make. I simply take a shower and get dressed.

Lunch Ready

I carry my lunch to work every day. I do this for three reasons: it saves money, it's usually healthier, and I don't have to leave my office or campus to find food. In the evening, I make sure that my lunch is ready to go for the next day.

Read

Whenever possible I try to read at least 30 minutes in the evening. This is usually a book on leadership, biography, or history. Sometimes, with the hectic schedule of having a family, this doesn't happen, but most days I do manage to carve out some time for daily reading.

Get Plenty of Sleep

This one, like daily exercise, meditation, and eating a good breakfast is backed by science (Barnes, 2018). If I am getting up at 4:00 in the morning, it's imperative that I go to sleep at an hour that gives me the seven or eight hours I need. Most nights, I am asleep by 9:00 p.m. If I don't get enough sleep, then I am setting myself up for a very difficult day.

Screen Time

Although this one isn't a routine, necessarily, I find it as important as the others on this list. It's the idea of taking time each day to disconnect from my phone and other screens. When I talk to the other leaders in my college about this, they all give me the same sort of look. It's the look that tells me that they can't imagine doing this. The "this" is to step away from our technology for a brief part of the day or the week. For me, I try to disconnect from my screens (phone and computer) at 5:00 p.m. each day. This doesn't mean that I never check messages or respond to emails, but 95% of the time, I don't. It allows my mind time to shut down and relax. It also allows me to focus my attention on other, more important things, like being a father to my son, and a husband to my wife.

The idea of disconnecting from my screens for part of the day or part of the week is an idea I picked up from Powers' (2011) book *Hamlet's Black-Berry*. In this book he describes the trappings of being constantly on call and being at the control of our devices. He advises that we should take en-tire days (for me it's usually a weekend day) to disconnect. Admittedly, this is more difficult for me now that I am a dean, but I still have this as a part of my weekly practice. Another book that speaks to this idea is Newport's *Deep Work: Rules for Focused Success in a Distracted World* (2016). Newport's book focuses on one central idea: that the work that we are required to do in the knowledge economy takes intense focus, and our environments (phones, computers, tablets) prevent us from being able to do this. This book is full of ideas about how to focus on your work and be more productive. Another book that looks at the impact that technology has on the current generation of teenagers (and our next cohort of students at universities) is Twenge's (2017) *iGen: Why Today's Super-Connected Kids are Growing Up Less Rebellious, More Tolerant, Less Happy—and Completely Unprepared for Adulthood.* Both of these books give us insight into the power that our personal devices have on our ability to navigate the world and our workplaces. For deans the pressure to be constantly on call and available is very real. My advice to new deans is to set realistic boundaries about your availability and willingness to commu-nicate with students, faculty, and other administrators. In my experience, there are very few things that can't wait until the next morning when you are at your desk.

"Hard to Form Words"

Taking care of yourself, whether through routines that simplify your day or stepping away from technology from time to time, is central to your success as a dean. Oftentimes when I read articles or hear people talk about the concept of self-care, it is framed as something that we should do, as some-thing that's optional. I don't take this approach. The strategies and ideas that I write about in this chapter are requirements for having the mental and physical effort to be a college dean. Perhaps others can do the job of dean and maintain their mental and physical well-being without these sorts of routines, but I am not one of them.

I am reminded of a phone call that I received one day when I was driving home from a day of teaching middle school and coaching middle school football. Those were some long but fulfilling days. My younger sister was calling about her day as a student teacher in an elementary school. Since I had been teaching for several years by this time, she was calling to decompress and ask for my advice on a couple things. Then the conversa-tion turned to the physical and mental strain that teaching a room full of elementary kids was taking on her. She said, "Do you ever get home in the evening, and it's like, you know, hard to form words?" That seemed like a weird question, so I asked her to clarify. "It's like, I am really tired at the end of the day, and I know what I want to say, but I can't get the right words to come out. It's hard to form words."

Yes. I knew what she was talking about. Being a new teacher is a lot like being a new dean. We feel this way because of information and decision overload. For the first month or two of my time as a new dean, I felt this way every day. For me, this feeling was usually combined with a headache or other physical sign of fatigue. I can recall several instances during the first three months of being dean in which I couldn't remember simple things that I had never had trouble remembering. I know this sounds strange, and probably even stranger to share these thoughts in a book about being a new dean. One day it was my office phone number. I couldn't remember it when someone asked me. Yes, the phone number in my email signature that I see every day. Another time, it was my zip code. I was filling out some paperwork, and I couldn't remember this. Then there was the time I was buying groceries and couldn't remember the PIN for my debit card. There I stood at the end of a busy day of being a dean, buying some items for dinner, unable to remember the four numbers required to make the purchase (I did eventually remember the numbers). Like I told my sister that day, yes. I know the feeling, and it's normal. It's something that you will adjust to. For me, this adjustment period was aided by routines and self-care.

Setting Expectations

I found that one of the most empowering parts of being a dean is that you (maybe for the first time) get to set workplace expectations for other people. This doesn't mean that you, alone, get to set the rules for everyone, but it does mean that the way that you carry yourself, the things that you respond to, and the way that you respond, sends messages to the entire college about how you see your role. If a faculty member sends an email to the entire faculty about something that they are displeased with, and you, as the dean, don't chime in to squash the discussion, you are sending the message that you are comfortable with faculty discussing issues in public. If you don't email faculty and staff at all hours of the day and night, you are sending the message that you see a strict division between personal time and work time. If you refuse to participate in gossip, you are sending the message that this sort of behavior is not something you are willing to tolerate. If you hold faculty to the promotion and tenure guidelines, you are sending the message that in order to be promoted and tenured, you must meet the guidelines and be a productive member of the team. As dean, when you speak or act, it's always more than just speaking and acting. Your speech and actions carry more weight.

With this in mind, I have very specific expectations for faculty and myself when it comes to emailing and communicating during the evening and on weekends. I was explicit about this in our first college meeting. My message was clear. I don't email faculty and staff at night, on weekends, or when the university is closed. In my opinion, this time belongs to the faculty and staff, not the dean and not the university. It has the effect of giving others the permission that they need to take this stance themselves. Setting this expectation also has an added benefit for me. In respecting others' time, they in turn, respect my time, and I am not bombarded with panicked emails at 10:30 at night. This helps to manage my own workload. When I get emails from faculty about issues, it's almost always during the workday, not at midnight.

Another area where I have tried to set expectations for the college is around complaining. Notice I said that I have "tried" to do this, because I am not always successful with this one. More specifically, I am talking about complaining in public to faculty and staff. I separate public complaining from private venting to a trusted colleague. The former is counter-productive; the latter is necessary. Faculty members (myself included) can be complainers. In fact, one of the difficult aspects of leading a group of people with terminal degrees is that we are, in a way, trained to see how things won't or can't work. We are, in the process of our academic training, schooled in the art of being skeptical and cautious. That is the nature of scientific inquiry. So, this comes out in our work. A certain degree of complaining is natural. But complaining can become a default position that prevents us from seeing possible solutions. As the dean, if you are complaining all the time, you are sending the message that this behavior is the standard, the norm. Complaining from the dean has a ripple effect. When you do it, others are given license to do it as well.

Instead of complaining, what if our default was, "How can we fix this?" Remember from Chapter 1, that I believe that one of the primary roles of a dean is to create an environment where talented people can do great things. Reducing complaining is a major part of that effort, and it all starts with you. Every problem that we have in a college is not an emergency. In fact, very few problems that we have in colleges are emergencies. But, you wouldn't know it from the way that some people behave when problems arise. Many times, this behavior is in response to the ways that the leadership behaves and talks about the problem. They are not only responding to the problem; they are responding to your response. They are responding to your response. If calm, rational behavior directed towards fixing problems (instead of panicking and complaining) is the norm, then faculty response will largely be the same. Faculty take their cue from the leadership team, so ensure that your leadership team can differentiate problems from emergencies and respond accordingly. A dean I used to work for had an expression that I have always remembered when it comes to setting the environment for problem solving. He used to say, "We don't work for NORAD." Of course, NORAD is the North American Aerospace Defense Command in Colorado Springs, CO. NORAD was created during the Cold War to monitor and respond to any incoming missile attacks from the Soviet Union. The images conjured by this organization are people who are on constant watch over the United States, standing vigilant against all threats and dangers, should they arise. As important as the work is that we do in colleges of education, it does not rise to the level of urgency as monitoring intercontinental ballistic missiles from our global enemies. The problem can wait until the morning. We don't work for NORAD.

Tell the Truth. Always

> *If it's not right, don't do it. If it's not true, don't say it.*
> —Marcus Aurelius

For this last section, I'd like to return to the ancient idea of Stoicism that I mentioned in Chapter 4. I include this in a chapter on self-care because, as the ancients pointed out, betraying your ethics and virtue harms not only the people it's directed at—it harms you as well. A line from Marcus Aurelius' Meditations (2002) sums this up, "To do harm is to do yourself harm. To do an injustice is to do yourself an injustice—it degrades you" (p. 119). I believe that we all know this to be true. When we wrong others, it sets the stage for bad things to happen to ourselves in the future, whether through revenge or by creating tension with those you work with. It's a cause and effect chain with a predictable (negative) outcome.

In addition to maintaining focus on the things we can actually change (as opposed to things that are outside of our control), Stoicism rests on the ideas of striving for virtue and employing reason to ascertain how to live a good life (Pigliucci, 2017). Part of taking care of yourself is tied to how we treat others: "... to live this life out truthfully and rightly. And, be patient with those who don't" (Aurelius, 2002, p. 80).

Of all the things about leadership that I have written about so far, I believe that integrity is the most important. I say this because I have experienced this during my first year, and I have experienced this throughout my career. I almost didn't include these thoughts in this book because I thought that it might come across as a sanctimonious lecture. That is not my intention. My intention is to share, from my experiences, how this basic idea applies to true leadership. It's something we've been told since we were little kids. Tell the truth. Honesty is the best policy. Integrity matters. It turns out that it was true then, and it's true now. In leadership, this basic ethical idea is the most important thing we do.

Let's imagine a scenario that could be in any organization. Picture the leader of the organization giving her people a talk about how she'd like to see the organization grow and flourish in the future. In this talk to the employees or faculty group, the new leader talks about her leadership style, the goals for the college, and how she handles the day-to-day operation of the organization. In fact, this is the sort of talk that new leaders give before they start a new job (usually in the interview process) and once they actually get the job (the first time they meet with people). The topics that are covered are predictable. I think they are predictable because new leaders intuitively know what people want to hear. They want to hear about the new leader's ideas for the future, a bit about past experiences, and if the new leader is approachable. It's a talk to answer the burning question: What kind of person will lead us?

I have heard leaders give these sorts of talks before, as I am sure you have too. We get a new dean or provost, and this person goes around to the different units to talk and get to know people. It's an introduction to them as a leader and a person. And, it's that last part that, for some people, is more important than the leader part. What kind of person are you? Now imagine a dean talking to her leadership team, or a provost talking to the college deans, or a president talking to his executive council. Imagine the messages that the leaders pass on to their closest circle of advisors and co-leaders. The messages to these groups largely follow the same topic and tenor, but are usually more specific, more granular to the job of running a college or university.

Imagine this dean or provost or president saying the following:

> More than anything I do or say to you from this point forward, I want you to all know something about me. I want you to remember this so when people ask you about me, you can tell them. You won't have to think of something to say, because you heard it directly from me. This is what you can tell people about the new guy. Nothing is more important to me than being ethical in our dealings with one another and with our stakeholders. We do the right things. We tell the truth. We behave ethically. If you can't do this, you can't serve with me. Nothing is more important than this. We will do some good

things together. We will have some successes and failures together, but these will occur standing on a foundation of integrity.

What sort of impact would this have on the people you serve, and by extension, the people they serve?

We don't follow people we don't trust. They might outwardly appear to follow you, but they don't. What you have gotten yourself is compliance. When we behave in ways that destroy the trust of our people we have created an environment in which the potential and talent of your people is diminished.

Establishing a culture of trust with the people you work with is the foundation on which everything else rests. Set the tone for the people in your organization that you will do the right things, that you will be honest, and that you seek good in your relationships with them. Choose this path for your college, and the stage will be set for great things to happen.

Reservoir of Trust

The interactions that we have with people function to build trust—or destroy trust. When we are working with people within the university structure, whether they are people in your college or not, people come to know you as someone they can trust or someone who is not to be trusted. How you are perceived—as either trustworthy or not—operates, as James Comey (2018) writes, like a reservoir. It takes longer to build trust than it does to lose it. In his book, he was writing about the integrity of the FBI and the Justice Department, but I think the same ideal can apply to the ways we operate in higher education. This idea that integrity and trustworthiness matter above all else. Everything we do rests on being able to trust that people in your organization to do the right thing.

> I told them it was a reservoir of trust and credibility built for you and filled for you by people you never knew . . . A reservoir that makes possible so much of the good that is done by the institution you serve . . . this one comes with a responsibility, a solemn obligation to guard and protect that reservoir and pass it on to those who follow as full as you received it, or maybe even fuller. I would explain that the problem with reservoirs is that they take a very long time to fill but they can be drained by one hole in the dam. The actions of one person can destroy what it took hundreds of people to build. (p. 54)

Perhaps you have seen this idea in action. Those days when someone you work with does the wrong thing in a given situation. They lie, or cheat, or deceive to get the upper hand. Sometimes it's you that's on the receiving end of this behavior, sometimes you aren't. But whether or not it's your trust that's broken is not the point. Observing people do the wrong thing to others has the same effect. If your supervisor or colleague would be dishonest in one situation, it tells you that the same behavior could be directed at you. During my time in higher education, I can remember losing trust in people that I worked with and some who I worked for. The overwhelming majority of the time, the people who I lost trust in, never regained it. In these cases, they refused to own their mistakes and make it right. Instead, they deflected, made excuses, and explained away their bad behavior. I am sure that you can think of episodes from your career, but the specifics don't really matter. The result was probably the same. What did you think about these episodes? How did they change your perception of the person? Did they increase the likelihood that you would trust them, or were you always wondering if they were being honest with you?

The answers to these questions are self-evident. The results are not surprising. Behaving this way undermines your efforts to lead and to do great things. Talking to your leadership team and the college about integrity is the first step towards creating a healthy and ethical atmosphere within your organization. Don't assume that people know this about you already. Be explicit and tell them. Express your desire to have integrity and an ethical outlook on the work we are here to do. Imagine how much mental space we'd all have if we reclaimed that part of our day in which we wondered if our colleagues were being ethical. If we stopped wasting time on trivial matters and focused on important work. This answer is self-evident as well. Integrity is good for us.

Do Good and Be Good—At the Same Time

> *Waste no more time arguing about what a good man should be. Be one.*
> —Marcus Aurelius

It is from my experiences that people intuitively know whether the people that lead them are doing the right things. When new leaders come in to an organization, they are tasked with doing good things for the organization. They are asked by their bosses or supervisors to increase enrollment or start a new program or set out to accomplish something that's never been done before. We have all seen this happen. People in leadership positions are routinely evaluated and assessed by their people (and their bosses) by how well they follow through with these tasks. If you are brought in, as a dean, to help with obtaining accreditation for your college, and you are able to secure it during your tenure, you are viewed as being a success. If you are tapped to begin new programs, and you are able to propose and establish these programs, then good for you. All of this is pretty normal. We are called on to do good things. Good things for our organizations. For me, this means doing good things with the help of the people in the college. I think we make a mistake when we put the accomplishment of these goals above the people that we serve, which is common in higher education.

We should be able to do good things and be good, at the same time. That means that we should be able to accomplish our collective goals and take care of our people at the same time. We should be able to accomplish these lofty goals and be ethical in the process. We should be able to do what we need to do and tell the truth. We should be able to make changes in our organizations and be honest with one another. We should be able to develop new ways of doing things and not treat people as expendable. In my career, I have found that the accomplishment of a big goal sometimes overshadows how we treat our people in the process. In fact, we begin to see the goal as more important than the people who are working on the goal. In this environment, we cut corners, lie, and deceive stakeholders during the process. We play games and tell people what they want to hear to ensure that we get what we want. People are viewed as being disposable in the process, as long as the big goal is accomplished. We allow the goal to overshadow what really matters—the people we serve. If the people we work with are sacrificed in the process of accomplishing our goals, what have we gained? Public accolades. What have we lost in this process? Our reputations and our word as bond. The former is temporary. The latter is forever.

I believe that we sometimes behave this way in higher education because it's more expedient. It's just easier to lie and deceive to get our way. To explain things and be honest takes more time. It takes more patience. It probably takes more effort to get buy-in from your people. Yes. Doing good while simultaneously being good is not always easy. But, we can do it. We can do good and be good, at the same time.

Philosophical and Practical

The good news about being an ethical person and always telling the truth is that this practice is the right thing to do and it helps you accomplish your goals. Again, I think that people who do not behave ethically believe that it works in the other direction—that dishonesty is a shortcut to getting what they want. It does appear this way. Sometimes. People tell half-truths, cut corners, and behave in unethical ways to get something done. The ends always justify the means. When it's all said and done, the person has something to show for his work. In a sense, you can see how this behavior, although not our best moment, did get something accomplished. But, what have you lost in the process? How does this impact how people see you and how you will accomplish future goals? The answer to this is simple. It will be harder.

When I read and reread drafts of this chapter, I came away thinking that I was sounding too religious or too philosophical. There are definitely aspects of both of these areas, but that wasn't my objective. What I am describing is a practical and pragmatic consideration of leading others. Yes. It's nice to tell the truth. Yes. It's the ethical thing to do. But, it also ensures that you will get more done as well. It's the right thing to do, and it makes your practical, pragmatic attempts at leadership easier. Religious and ethical codes demand it, and it's good for your practice as a leader.

The take away here is clear. Be good so you can do good. Your efforts at leading others depend on it.

References

Anderberg, J. (2017, September 12). *Make every day a good day with this morning routine.* Retrieved from https://www.artofmanliness.com/2017/09/12/make-every-day-good-day-morning-routine/

Art of Manliness. (2015, July 17). *The Power of Morning & Evening Routines | The Art of Manliness* [Video file]. Retrieved from https://www.youtube.com/watch?v=lSKpu_qGMH4

Aurelius, M. (2002). *Meditations.* New York, NY: The Modern Library.

Barnes, C. (2018). Sleep well, lead better. *Harvard Business Review,* (September–October). 140–143. Retrieved from https://hbr.org/2018/09/sleep-well-lead-better?

Comey, J. (2018). *A higher loyalty: Truth, lies and leadership.* New York, NY. Flatiron Books.

Henk, B., Wepner, S., Lovell, S., & Melnick, S. (2017). Education deans' beliefs about essential ways of thinking, being, and acting: A national survey. *Journal of Education Management, 32*(1), 195–213.

Kabat-Zinn, J. (2005). *Coming to our senses: Healing ourselves and the world through mindfulness.* New York, NY: Hachette Books.

Newport, C. (2016). *Deep work: Rules for focused success in a distracted world.* New York, NY: Hatchette Books.

Pigliucci, M. (2017). *How to be a stoic: Using ancient philosophy to live a modern life.* New York, NY: NY: Basic Books.

Powers, W. (2011). *Hamlet's BlackBerry: Building a good life in the digital age.* New York, NY: Harper Perennial.

Robbins, J. H., & Schmitt, D. M. (1994, February). Who is leading us toward quality professional development? Paper presented at the annual meeting of the American Association of Colleges for Teacher Education, Chicago.

Spall, B., & Xander, M. (2018). *My morning routine: How successful people start everyday inspired.* New York, NY: Routledge.

Twenge, J.M. (2017). *iGen: Why today's super-connected kids are growing up less rebellious, more tolerant, less happy—and completely unprepared for adulthood.* New York, NY: Atria Books.

8

Trust People

The lone-warrior model of leadership is heroic suicide. Each of us has blind spots that require the vision of others. Each of us has passions that need to be contained by others. Anyone can lose the capacity to get on the balcony, particularly when the pressures mount. Every person who leads needs help in distinguishing self from role and identifying the underlying issues that generate attack.

—Ronald Heifetz (1994, p. 268)

BIG IDEA FOR THIS CHAPTER

As a new dean, the learning curve is steep. There is so much that you don't know about your new institution that you are forced to lean on others for help and assistance. In this process, being able to trust people is key. For me, this was trusting the leadership team to help me make decisions; by extension, I was asking them to trust the people in their areas as well. Their help took the form of listening to me brainstorm solutions and pointing me in the right

BIG IDEA

direction. In order for this relationship to be established, I had to trust those around me. This is a particularly difficult thing to do as the new person. I went from being knowledgeable about the way things worked (at my previous job) to not knowing much of anything about the terms, structures, and people in my new university. In this process, I was forced to examine my default positions on a variety of issues and surrender to the idea of vulnerability as essential part of leading a college.

It seems that many of the leaders (and professors for that matter) I have been around see the world through a binary lens. They see their work and the interactions with people as being and existing on one end of a binary spectrum of good or bad. This seems to be more pronounced among leaders, perhaps because they are in the business of working closely with people to accomplish difficult goals. Leading people is a difficult endeavor and this causes us to distrust the people with whom we work. Perhaps this is natural. We tend to remember the leadership episodes in which we were deceived or when things didn't go so well with a colleague. Painful experiences have a way of affixing themselves to our working memory. Being lied to or deceived or double-crossed has a way of overtaking many of the good things that happen to us. When this happens, these experiences become the filter through which we view future interactions. But, what if it didn't have to be that way? What if we minimized the bad and remembered the good? This may sound naive, but this is what I am suggesting. What if instead of assuming the worst in people, we assumed the best? If we are always looking for the negative and seeking out problematic behavior, then that is what we tend to find and focus on. Simply put, we find what we look for. So the stance is simple: if you want to find more good, start looking for more good. This starts with trusting people to do the right things.

What Do You Think? (Revisited)

It's a simple concept. When you are an external hire for a dean's position, you are put in a position of having the least amount of institutional knowledge while simultaneously having the most power within your college. With this power comes the tendency of people to ask you questions seeking your approval for ideas and projects. Sometimes they are asking your opinion because they want to do something in a different way. The way you respond to these types of questions sends messages to your faculty and gives them insight into the kind of leader you will be. I have always thought that, given my newness to this role and given that I have less institutional knowledge than just about everyone in the college, my default answer to questions would be the same regardless of who was asking the question. Sometimes faculty would ask about starting a new program (see Chapter 3) or inquire about possible changes to protocol. Sometimes staff who play a major role in our licensing and field experience offices would ask about how we collect information or communicate with students. My response was always the same.

What Do You Think?

In my default question, I am not giving permission to do any of those things. Yet. Simply giving someone permission to do something in a college, with little background on how things work (because I am new), is lazy and shortsighted. I am more interested in why someone thinks we should do something or change something or try something. Usually the person asking the question has partially or fully worked out the problem in their head.

Having this as a default answer to most questions also reveals something to your people that is more powerful than a simple question. You are telling your people that you trust their judgment and that their ideas are valuable. This does not mean that every time someone asks you to do something you say, "What do you think? Really? That's a great idea. Let's do that." That is not what I am saying. I am saying that in a college you have highly educated and highly knowledgeable and experienced faculty and staff working with you everyday. They know stuff. And since they know stuff, you should tap into that expertise whenever you can. The most fascinating part of this question (and where it sometimes leads) is the look that comes over the faces of people who are asked, "What do you think?" For some, it's like they've never been asked this question by someone in a position of authority. It's like they don't understand the question, and if they do understand, they have a look of distrust or doubt. For others, perhaps it is the first time that anyone has asked them this question in a work setting.

I have been in leadership situations in the past where the higher-ups in the organization criticized and lamented the innovation or work of the faculty. They would often talk about how faculty lacked initiative or the will to take responsibility for their units or programs. When I reflect on these situations, these departments and colleges were so top down in nature that the faculty had no ownership of the processes that ran the unit. Inherent in this way of operating is a fundamentally negative outlook on the faculty or employees. For many in leadership, the goal of being a leader is to get people to follow them. They want to create more followers. The irony of this goal is that if you are successful, you have created people who are solely dependent on your ideas and your judgment. With this comes the expectation that you will give and take away permission, that you will make the call on all decisions, and that you (and you alone) are invested in the creation of solutions. How apropos that leaders get frustrated when no one will develop innovative ideas, when they are the only one making decisions and judging ideas.

I am suggesting that this way of treating your faculty as a way of attempting to lead them is wrongheaded. If we want people to take responsibility for their areas, to solve problems, to be innovative, and to trust one another, we should empower them. We don't want to create more followers. As leaders, we want to create more leaders.

What Are Your Default Positions?

When we make decisions, we are broadcasting our priorities to the world. You can tell a lot by someone's value system by looking at where people spend their time and by the decisions they make. And it's not just about the things that people (and colleges) decide to do. There is also explanatory power in the things that we decide to not do. How we approach issues within our colleges and the decisions that we make are outward manifestations of our belief systems. With this in mind, it is helpful to think about your default positions. Your default position on a given subject or aspect of your job is the point at which you start thinking about how to approach the problem, issue, or aspect of your life as dean. It's simply the starting point. I think that we overemphasize the finality of some of our decisions at the expense of thinking of the front end of our decision-making. With leadership, there is a tendency to fixate on the solutions and how they signal the end of something, the end of the problem, the end of the issue. We even use the phrase "at the end of the day" to explain how we frame solutions to problems. We say things like, "Well. At the end of the day nothing matters except how many students we are able to get enrolled." With this move, we are discounting all of the possible actions and thoughts that come before we make a decision. This line of thinking assumes that there are no stances we should take a priori, that we should only focus on the end. I disagree. I think that our starting point for making decisions and the stances that we take, can help us filter good solutions from better solutions. It can also help us to simplify things. Instead of having to make reactive decisions about a myriad of issues (which is exhausting), having some default positions about things gives us a starting point from which to operate.

Your default positions operate much like the mission statement of a college or university. Think of the mission statements that you've seen. It's usually a pithy statement about the college's beliefs followed by three to five sub-statements that shed light on what the college is about. Ideally, mission statements are put forth as a way to help the institution make strategic decisions about who they are, who they want to be (aspirational), and what principles they stand for. It helps the institution frame their future actions. When confronted with a decision to make, college and university leaders can simply ask themselves: Is this who we are? Does this fit with our mission as an institution? Is this action in line with our beliefs? If the answer to those three questions is "yes," you are making decisions with your beliefs as a default position. The mission statement serves as a tool to filter out the initiatives and ideas that aren't in line with who you are and what you represent. When we make decisions without considering who we are (as a dean, college, or university), we are in danger of making decisions that are not only misaligned with our beliefs, but decisions that tend to address short term issues and concerns. What is good for us in the short term, isn't always good for us in the long term.

As a dean, the same can be said for our personal default positions. What is your personal mission statement? What are the commitments that you strive to keep? Having a handful of default positions can help you navigate the minefield of decision-making in the dean's office. This doesn't mean that you rigidly follow some code of beliefs, but rather that you have thought through and adhere to a baseline of ideals when it comes to specific topics. It's also useful to have explicit conversations with your leadership team about your default positions and have them discuss theirs. In this way, you are more on the same page with one another in meetings when decisions are being discussed. If you do this, you will be coming to the table with a basic understanding of where people stand on the issues.

As you think through your default stances, ask yourself about your orientation to the following categories of interaction within your college. What is your default position when it comes to:

Faculty/Staff: How do you see the work of faculty and staff? Do you have a positive or negative view of the ways in which faculty work is organized, rewarded, structured, and carried out? As a leader, do you see faculty/staff as an asset?

Why It Matters: The work of your college is performed by your faculty and staff. If you have a negative view of the faculty and staff, how is this negativity being reflected to them? Faculty and staff want to own the work of the college, just make sure that you aren't creating conditions that make this harder. This happens when you don't see your faculty and staff as assets. They are literally on the front lines of all that takes place in your College. If you have negative views of your faculty and staff, ask yourself why.

Faculty Governance: How do you view the idea of faculty governance in your college? Do you trust faculty and staff to be able to make the right decisions within the context of existing faculty governance structures? Or are faculty not to be trusted when it comes to making decisions?

Why It Matters: Faculty (again) want ownership of the their college and be involved in making decisions. The culture around this idea varies across universities, but I have literally never heard someone say "I really wish they'd exclude us more from decision making and shared governance." Since you like to be involved in shared governance and since you like to be in the loop on decisions, extend the same courtesy to the people you are trying to lead.

The Purpose of a University: How do you see the work of the university in the context of the larger world? What are we here for? Are we here for workforce and economic reasons? Are we here for the development of people to become more fully human? Both? Something else?

Why It Matters: The university landscape is changing, and has undergone drastic changes in the past 30 years. The most obvious manifestation of these changes is the way in which state funding for higher education has decreased to reflect a narrower purpose of what we do. Although I don't believe that most faculties at universities adhere to this line of thinking, it is a reality that we must face. Understanding what modern universities are about helps to frame the big picture for leaders when it comes to decision-making.

Your Work is Important: Do you think that the work you do in your college is important for reasons larger than the here and now? If so, can you verbalize why you think it's important?

Why It Matters: Being able to verbalize this idea has helped me throughout my career. Once or twice a year, I reflect on my personal and professional goals that I have. When I have asked my leadership team about their goals, they are often uncomfortable with the idea that faculty should have personal and professional goals. I think this emotion comes from the fact that this question is rarely asked by leadership. Having goals and believing our work is important is what sustains us. It gives us direction. Without it, we are adrift.

Students: How do you see your students? Are they customers coming to you for a service? Are they coming to you for professional development? In your mind, do they add to or take away from your daily work? Are they an asset to what you do or a distraction and/or problem?

Why It Matters: How we frame students allows us to contextualize and frame everything else. How we view our relationship with students sets the stage for how we interact with and serve them.

Other Leaders: Are other leaders and deans in your university reservoirs of knowledge or are they your competitors for resources in a game of politics? Do you work with or do you work against other leaders in your university? This might be worth bringing up the next time you all meet.

Why It Matters: Leadership at the dean's level need not be a zero-sum game of winners and losers. Much more can be accomplished through collaboration and cooperation than by cutthroat competition. It should also be noted that not all colleges have the same access to internal and external resources, so the playing field isn't level to begin with. For example, colleges of education don't attract the same kinds of external funding as say, a college of medicine or STEM.

Information: How do you view the distribution of information? Is it something that is to be protected and guarded for a few people, or do you feel that it's better for as many people as possible to know about things in your college? Do you intentionally withhold or share information with others? What sort of environment does this cause?

Why It Matters: Decisions are made on the basis of information. If you are the only one with information, then that sends the message that you are the only one with good ideas or that you are the sole decider on all issues. Conversely, if you share information as necessary, you are sending the message that others have much to contribute and that they have a voice in making decisions.

Your Leadership Style: Do you have a leadership style or model that you adhere to? There are lots of books and articles on different leadership styles and models (list of books from Chapter 2). As I have said earlier, my default is Buller's *Positive Academic Leadership* (PAL) (2013). Are you reacting to your day or do you have a model that you proactively follow?

Why It Matters: Having a style or a set of leadership principles to follow allows you to simplify your existence as a leader. When confronted with an issue or when planning how to lead, I simply refer to or think about the aspects of PAL (Chapter 1). This doesn't mean that every issue or dilemma can be solved with this leadership idea, but that's not the point. Leadership is not about having a list of the top ten leadership moves or ideas. The reason is simple. Leadership is too complex and too difficult to be decided by a checklist. Instead of a checklist, broad ideas about how to lead are the key. These broad ideas help you to filter every day occurrences, decisions, and actions.

Trust: Do you trust the people around you, or do you distrust the people around you?

Why It Matters: Trusting your leadership team and your faculty is the starting point for all good work in your college. Perhaps we make this one harder than it has to be. Think about yourself and how you want to be perceived for a moment: Do you want to be trusted by the people you work with? Or do you want people to distrust and always think the worst about you? We both know the answer to this. Trusting people is the default stance on which all of the others rest. It's the standard default. The golden rule of leadership. Trust people, assume the best, and allow people to try and fail. There is a chance that you will be deceived and/or disappointed, and that's OK. I have found that the odds that someone will do the right thing greatly outweigh the people who will do the wrong things. In this case, I'd rather be proven wrong than proven right.

"It's Like We've Been Walking Around in the Dark"

Trust involves more than just treating people with respect. For my first year as a dean, one of the first things I wanted to establish was the idea that sharing information with the leadership team was going to be the way that I conducted business. My default stance when it came to information was to share, not withhold, information with the team. The other aspect of working with the leadership team that I emphasized was that we would be learning new ways of doing things, together. Since we had new positions and since the group was newly formed, we would all be learning together. To this end, I was always sending the team articles on leadership strategy. These ideas (articles, books, videos, etc.) became a part of our meetings. In a way, our leadership team consisted of smart, accomplished people who were leading their own areas (departments, assessment, teacher education, licensure, staff) in isolation and without regard for the other areas. They were not in the habit of considering how their actions and decisions might impact the larger college. They needed to be invited to the table. Once they had been invited to the table, and once the default position of sharing information was established, the work of running the college could begin. I saw my role as the dean as a leader of leaders. And so I discussed issues and framed decisions with this idea in mind.

Leadership thinker Simon Sinek (2017) has a line that I think fits perfectly with this idea: "Be the leader you wish you had" (p. 288). If we allow this simple idea to guide our leadership behaviors, we are more likely to do the right things. At one of our meetings, a member of the leadership team noticed the shift in the way information was being shared for the good of the entire college. She commented on the readings that the group was considering, and said something that sums up what I think leadership looks like. Referring to the shared readings for that meeting she said, "Thanks for all of this. Before all of this, it's like we've been walking around in the dark." I can still remember the feeling that came over me when she said this: it's like we've been walking around in the dark. That weekend, I went and bought everyone on the leadership team a cheap $1 flashlight as a reminder that we weren't doing that anymore. That's a good way to reflect on your leadership and the people with whom you work. Are you having people stumble around in the dark, unsure of where they are going, unsure of the goals, and working in isolation? Or, do your people have a light to lead the way? Be the leader you wish you had. Turn the lights on.

Culture, Change, and Improvement

Every college has a culture. There are cultures around how faculty treat one another, how faculty view their work, and even how people dress. There are unspoken cultural norms around how people view the leader. Culture is sometimes hard to pick up because it's just the way things are done, so it seems automatic and common sense. This is what makes culture so hard to perceive and to change. French philosopher and sociologist Pierre Bourdieu (1977) called this idea habitus, the idea that our cultural habits and ways we see the world are reinforced by our experiences in a given setting. These habits and ways of seeing the world are reinforced by the ways in which we interact with the world—creating the illusion that these cultural dispositions are normal. Of course, our cultures aren't common sense or normal. This is clear when you, as an outsider to a culture, enter into that culture. Outsiders see the normal culture of a group with different eyes. As an externally hired new dean, this is a daily occurrence. What seems normal to the group is, in fact, not that normal to you. At all. This isn't a judgment about good or bad, or right and wrong. Culture can be either of these things.

The main point when it comes to culture is that there are aspects of the culture that you, as the dean, have some control over. You will have more control over certain areas of your college than others, and it takes time to shift a culture. Three areas that I believe that deans have control over is how people view the nature of change, the nature of success, and being able to admit their mistakes (vulnerability loop). I believe that having honest stances about these three areas can transform the way that people view their jobs and their relationship to one another.

To start with, I believe that leaders should have a realistic view of change. When new leaders start their new positions and begin to talk about change, they are looking to improve the ways things are done. They aren't changing aspects of the college to make things worse; they are changing things in the college because they perceive a need to do things in a different, but better way. Because the new leader is not ensconced in the existing culture, the solutions put forth by the new leader seem reasonable to her. In fact, one causes the other: the common sense of the new leader's ideas seems to be common sense because of a lack of cultural connection to this group. This too is normal. If you are new to a culture, then it makes sense that you'd have little connection and attachment to the way they do things. This is where the trouble begins. Leaders who strive to change things without reference to the ways in which people view the organization tend to oversimplify things. I know that I am guilty of this. The oversimplification of change looks like Figure 8.1. New leaders come to the new culture and see change and improvement like Figure 8.1.

This is what we imagine change to look like. Figure 8.1 (and the two that follow) was created by my associate dean to share with our faculty during a college wide meeting. The ideas we have are so obvious to us that we are actually taken by surprise when other people don't agree with us and

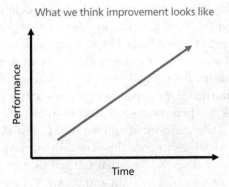

What we think improvement looks like

Figure 8.1

tell us that our idea for change is great. We are surprised because we don't know the context and history of the people on the front lines of making this change. I believe that one of the first things we should do as new leaders—before we begin to initiate change—is to get some consensus about whether or not there is something to be fixed or improved upon. When I perceived that there was an area that we needed to change or that needed to be improved upon, I almost always took the idea to my leadership team. I did this for several reasons. First, I wanted to make sure that I was seeing what I thought I was seeing. It is possible be believe that you are 100% correct in seeing an issue for what it represents. It is also possible to feel 100% confident (in your mind) of your stance and be 100% wrong. This is where your leadership team comes in. They are in a position to tell you how accurate your assessment of a given situation is. In fact, it's ideal when people on your leadership team see an issue in different ways because it highlights that issues are often more complicated than they seem at first glance. Second, your leadership team can point out things you haven't considered. Because they have more context than you and because they represent different (more specialized) areas than you, they know where the landmines are located. Ask your team, "What am I missing? Are there things I am not thinking about? Any unforeseen consequences of making this change? Are there reasons why this won't work?"

Few changes are universally liked or have no negative consequences on anyone. There are changes that people feel make their job better, and there are changes that people feel make their job worse. Often, the same change can have both results, depending on who you are. I prefer that my leadership team give me honest answers to these questions before I make a change, rather than being surprised later. Third, my leadership team helped me think about how to best communicate to faculty and how to implement changes. Most faculty I have worked with are particularly irritated when changes are made that impact them, and they aren't given prior notice or prior consultation. Leaders in colleges should take the time and make an effort to communicate potential changes to faculty. Ideally, there should be levels of consultation with people whom the changes will impact. For my first year as dean, changes usually went through the leadership team, department chairs, departments (via departmental meetings), and discussion at the full college level (see Chapter 10). This allowed multiple levels of the college to consider, discuss, and decide these issues. I believe that most, but not all, decisions in a college should have mechanisms like this in place when decisions are made that impact the entire group.

Another aspect of driving change that is difficult for new leaders is represented in the graph below. Even if we communicate change to our faculty in an efficient manner, and even if we seek and obtain consensus from multiple levels of the college, change and improvement is still hard. Even if your idea for improvement is a good one, that doesn't mean that it will be easy to implement. In fact, your college (or other unit) will most likely struggle with change at the beginning. Even when changes start off on a good foot and seem to be working, it might be that the other shoe hasn't fallen yet. What starts out as progress and improvement over the first days tapers off. Following this tapering off is a period in which things seem worse than they did before the change was made. That's the dip that you see in Figure 8.2. The dip is the period when the newness of the change wears off and people pine for the old ways of doing things. The dip is where the rubber meets the road when it comes to you and your leadership team's ability to listen, adjust, and evolve. During the dip, things feel worse than before. That's the way that these emotions are interpreted by people going through the change. It's not that things are actually worse, in fact, things may be getting better, more efficient, and more responsive. But, these changes feel harder because they are new. Although the standard way of doing things wasn't the best, at least it was known and routine. We like known and routine. And, during the dip period known and routine often sounds and feels better than unknown and new.

Taking the time with your leadership team, in department and college-wide meetings to address these feelings is a good idea. The gap between the known/routine and the unknown/new needs to be bridged by leadership in the college, at all levels. One of the things that our leadership team decided to do before a big change in our college was to show these graphs to the college as we implemented a big change. For one of our biggest changes, the implementation stage took place in March-April after discussing, debating, deciding, and adopting changes in September, October, November,

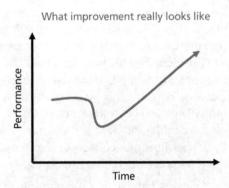

What improvement really looks like

Performance

Time

Figure 8.2

December, January, and February. During the implementation stage, we were explicit about how we expected the changes that we were trying to implement would take time, effort, and patience. In this way, we were prepping the faculty for the inevitable difficulty that comes with implementing change. In my experience, faculty prefer (as do I) to have an accurate assessment of the changes that are coming, rather than an overly optimistic version of how the leadership believes the change will unfold. This last part is about setting expectations. The message is clear: We have spent months discussing this change. The faculty has agreed it needs to happen (for us, it was a vote). It's time to implement the change. It won't be easy or seamless, but these improvements will make our college stronger.

The last visual that we used in our college meeting before we implemented our change was Figure 8.3.

This builds on the idea that in the short term, things aren't as easy as we'd like for them to be. We tend to frame improvement as something that happens automatically after a change is made, but that's not the way it works in complex organizations. Improvement brought about as a result of change is not an event. It's a process. As the visual bears out, a sometimes messy and frustrating process. Chances are that the issue that you are trying to improve took shape and evolved over time. The longer it's been in place, the more people have become attached to it. Attachment to ways of doing things in a college is normal, as is the frustration of changing these things. Be clear on why you are making changes, filter your ideas through the layers of your college, and then act. But realize that real improvement takes more than a good idea. Improvement takes time, patience, discussion, and the ability to communicate "why" to people. And, once you have these components in place make sure that you frame it as a process, not an event.

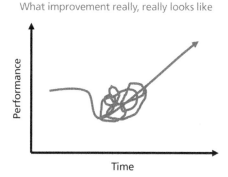

Figure 8.3

Apologize (Correctly)

I have a painting in my office that my mother gave me with these words, "Want the last word? Apologize." In my mind, there is another skill related to being able to share your vulnerability, and that is the ability to apologize correctly. Just as with the preceding section, some of the same ideas apply. Being vulnerable allows the rest of the team to do the same. Apologizing has the same effect. Apologizing for something you have said or done wrong allows people a blueprint to follow when they mess up. Which will happen. Without this template to follow, people act as if they are the only ones who need to apologize for things. That's never been the case with teams that work closely on difficult goals. Eventually something will be done or said for which someone needs to apologize. I am suggesting that as the leader, you should go first. As the leader, there is no need to send the message that you are always right, or that you have too much pride to apologize for your actions. With the stress of being the new dean combined with the lack of knowledge about your new university, there will be mistakes. Therefore, there will be opportunities to apologize. Sometimes it will be a simple oversight or technical mistakes that you have made, other times it will be for things you simply shouldn't have done to someone else. No one is immune from petty behavior. Social science research tells us that we are likely to assign negative motive to others' actions and lofty purposes for our own actions (Aronson, 2007). Everyone else is bad, and I am good—that's how we see ourselves. It is healthy to see ourselves for the bad actors we can sometimes be.

When I was a professor in Alabama, I was selected to chair a committee to revise the university's mission and vision statements. I was honored to chair this important committee, and was eager to do a good job. But it was a bit harder than I had anticipated. Apparently getting professors, administrators, and external stakeholders to agree to a succinct statement about the vision of a university isn't so simple. There were some bumps in the road for the first two or three meetings, but after I stopped talking so much and started listening, things began to come together. In the first phases of our work, I was increasingly frustrated with a person we will call Professor A. This person consistently and persistently told me that the ideas I had weren't going to work, and it appeared that he wanted the project to fail. I secretly hoped that he would miss our meetings so I wouldn't have to deal with him. It seemed to me that we could make some headway on our project if he wasn't always derailing the conversation with his negative comments. During the end of our first month of work, I got my wish. He missed one of our regular meetings. Predictably, we got more accomplished in an environment that was less combative and more cooperative. As I was clos-ing the meeting, one of the committee members commented on Professor A's absence and how things had gone smoothly during the meeting. This caused a nervous laugh from the committee members as I adjourned the meeting. And, then I did it. I couldn't help myself. As we were gathering up our belongings, I added to the previous comment about Professor A. I need not repeat it here, but I said something that I shouldn't have said. In fact, like a middle school kid, I called him a name. Out loud. In front of other people. The looks on their faces were ones of disbelief. Did he just say what I think he said? Yep. That was me. The chair of the committee. Not my proudest moment.

When everyone filed out of the room, I stayed behind and sat in one of the chairs around the table. I knew that it was highly likely that someone in that meeting would go to Professor A and tell him what I had just said. In fact, there was a 100% chance that that was going to happen. I kept thinking how stupid it was to have said that, in that setting, about that person. Stupid. I had gotten frustrated with the way things were going, and I lost my common sense for three seconds. I wish I hadn't said it, but I did. After about five minutes of self-flagellation, I made the decision that I would just go to the person's office and apologize, before anyone had a chance to tell him what happened. I knew he was on campus at another engagement during our meeting, so I walked over immediately to his office. When I arrived, his office door was open and he was typing something on his computer. I knocked.

"Come in. Oh. Dr. Chandler. What can I do for you?" he asked.

"We missed you at the meeting this morning..."

"Yeah, I had that thing with the curriculum committee. How'd the meeting go?"

Time to rip off the Band-Aid. "That's sort of why I came by. At the end of the meeting someone joked about how you weren't there and how work was easier. Then I called you a _____ (insert word of choice here). I shouldn't have said that. It was wrong. I apologize. I think I said it because it is sometimes frustrating in meetings when you disagree and shoot down every idea that I have. But, that's not an excuse. I am sorry for saying that. It won't happen again." In the span of an hour and a half, I had conducted a successful committee meeting, called someone a name, walked across campus, and apologized to the person I had wronged. Quite a busy morning.

The look on his face was one of confusion. He spoke, but the inflec-tion of his voice sounded like he was asking questions instead of making statements.

"Ok? Thanks for stopping by and letting me know…" It was awkward. At the first sign that the conversation had stalled, I took the opportunity to escape his office. As I walked back to my office, I felt like a fool. Not for what happened in his office, but for putting myself in that situation. Later in the day, he visited my office. My guess was that he was there to say something in his own defense, to ask why I had called him a name. I was wrong. He was there to thank me for apologizing, in person. He also said that no one had ever told him that he was difficult in meetings, and that it wasn't intentional. He didn't perceive his actions as being disruptive or disagreeable. He said that he would take cautions to be more helpful in meetings. It felt like I was in an alternate universe. The person who I had called a name in an open meeting was telling me that he would make an effort to not be difficult anymore. This is a lesson that I have never forgotten, and one that I told several times during my first year as dean. In fact, I told it during my interview before I got the job. Going directly to a person and apologizing for something you've done wrong is not a sign of weakness. It's also not as bad as people imagine it to be. Just follow this template: I am sorry for _____. I will work to make sure that it doesn't happen again. In my experience as an administrator, this works every time. It also has the added benefit of letting other people know that they can apologize when they do something wrong. It's a win-win for everyone. Just make sure that your apology is a real apology, not one of those situations where you do verbal gymnastics to make it sound like you are apologizing, but you are really doing something else. You know this has happened when you hear someone (or yourself) say something like, "I am sorry that you feel that way or I am sorry that I made you feel that way." If you feel the need to keep talking or to qualify your comments, just stop after the first three words. When it comes to apologizing, less is more.

There is no need to win every argument or to have the last word when it comes to dispute. You are going to be working with your faculty for the foreseeable future. Engage in behaviors, as the leader, which ensure that this relationship can be sustained over time. We do this by making sure that we apologize when we have wronged people. How many strained relationships and hurt feelings do you know of that exist in colleges because both sides are unwilling to say I am sorry? In leadership, being able to apologize and move on from mistakes is a superpower.

References

Aronson, E. (2007). *The social animal.* New York, NY: Worth.

Bourdieu, P. (1977). *Outline of a theory of practice.* Cambridge: Cambridge University Press.

Buller, J. (2013). *Positive academic leadership: How to stop putting out fires and start making a difference.* San Francisco, CA: Jossey-Bass.

Heifetz, R. (1994). *Leadership without easy answers.* Cambridge, MA: Harvard University Press.

Sinek, S. (2017). *Leaders eat last: Why some teams pull together and others don't.* New York, NY: Penguin Books.

$$9$$

Make it OK for People to Follow You

> *Become the kind of leader that people would follow voluntarily;*
> *even if you had no title or position.*
>
> —Brian Tracy

BIG IDEA FOR THIS CHAPTER

As a new dean, the ways in which people perceive you are varied. The lenses through which people view you and your actions are dependent on many things, some of which you have control over and others you don't. Some view your actions through the lens of previous deans; some view you through a pessimistic lens; some view you with optimism; some, who have been school leaders before, view you with patience and understanding, because they have literally been there before. These lenses are people's way of making sense of the world and the people with whom they interact. I have found that these default lenses people have about are hard to change (or to correct, if you think people are wrong about you). There are several ways that I have tried to connect with faculty, especially my leadership team, to get a better sense of how things in the college (myself included) are being perceived. I have used the ideas of vulnerability, followership, and metaphors to help people engage in leadership with me.

This chapter is about the relationship that you have with your faculty and with your leadership team. Leadership is about more than just knowing how things work and telling people what to do. There are many things that you, as a leader, cannot control. But there are many, I would argue, more important aspects about leadership that you can control. For me, this is an exciting idea—that the things which really matter in leadership are within our control to change, tweak, fix, or adjust. When I was a teacher educator, I used to tell my students that the most important parts of an educational system are the teachers that work within that system. That, of course, sounds obvious. The most important factor in the education of a child is the teacher that a child has. I believe the same is true for leaders of colleges. The way that you create, sustain, and support a positive culture, as the leader, is one of the most important factors in any successful college. I know this sounds obvious and common sense. But, in many cases this common sense is not that common. The opposite is true. In places where this is not true, staff, faculty, and leadership tend to focus on external factors as the culprit for their dysfunction. The root cause of the dysfunction is thought to be something that is being forced upon the group, and of course this can sometimes be true. But, what if we looked inward at our organizational culture and started with the idea that culture is what we make it? Our workplace culture is not simply foisted upon us while we helplessly flounder through the days, weeks, months, and years of our careers. The culture that we inhabit and navigate is of our own creation. We aren't helpless bystanders to the way that our college culture operates. Good or bad, our cultures are of our own creation. For toxic cultures and negative environments, we are to blame.

The good news is that it doesn't have to be that way. Small changes in the way that people relate to one another and to leadership make all the difference. In fact, the research on high performing group culture and emotional intelligence in groups backs this up. What matters are small actions that compound over time that serve to create powerful group cultures. Small actions that can be started by you, the dean.

Showing Your Weaknesses

What stands in the way becomes the way.
—Marcus Aurelius

What is your relationship with failure? I realize that this is a strange question for leaders. But, the fact that we find this question to be strange, is part of the problem. Most of us avoid talking about our failures because they point to some shortcoming that we have had in the past. We actively seek to minimize, deflect attention away from, and downplay the times where we've messed up, made a mistake, or dropped the ball. What if we took the opposite approach? How might that change the way that our colleges operate and how our people go about their work? I am proposing a counterintuitive relationship with the idea of failure and discussing this with your leadership team and faculty. What's the worst that could happen? People will realize that you have made mistakes too? That making mistakes is a part of being human? That mistakes are a fundamental part of doing complex work? Yes, yes, and yes. If that's where the power of this idea ended, we'd still be ahead of where we are now. I would argue there is more to gain from this than simply the realization that everyone makes mistakes. The thing that we gain? Trust in each other.

When I was a first-year assistant professor in Alabama, I was given a one course reduction in my teaching load, and I was placed on less demanding committees. This was my dean's way of easing me into the water as a new tenure track professor. One of the committees I was placed on was the "NCATE Documents Committee" (for the uninitiated, NCATE is the former accreditation council for colleges of education). My role here was simple. We had file folders in the basement of our building that had to be filled with evidence from our accreditation work. For instance, if a document was labeled or listed as a "Standard 1.4" document, my job was to take the document and literally place it in the appropriate folder. Sounds easy? It was. It had the added benefit of getting me out of my office where I could talk to and get to know other faculty members in the college. There would be designated times where several faculty members would go to the "document room" (aka the basement), and work on putting our evidence into the correct folders.

One afternoon there was an email sent out to the committee that they would be working on this task the following Monday afternoon, so I added this to my calendar. When the day arrived, I was in the basement working with the others, learning about the college from faculty, and feeling like I was contributing to the larger accreditation efforts, which to the new guy, seemed to be freaking everyone out. After eating pizza, talking to faculty, and working in the document room for two or three hours, I returned to my office to do other work. I noticed that I had about ten emails from students. At first glance, I thought that was odd. Until I started reading their emails. Students had emailed me from about 1:15 p.m. until about 2:00 p.m.. Their question? They were wondering where I was. I was supposed to meet my class that day at 1:00 p.m. They had showed up for class, but their professor had not. He was in the basement, filing papers into manila folders. Some were simple emails like "Did you cancel class today? We are here and wondering where you are…" Others were more panicked and serious, "We are all here ready for class to start. We hope you are okay…" I looked at my watch. The class was over. I had completely missed my own class. Way to make a good impression. In fact, I had forgotten that I was supposed to teach that day. I was so busy learning how to be a new assistant professor and wanting to make a good impression on my new colleagues, that my Monday afternoon class completely slipped my mind. My emotions were as follows: confusion (at the emails), realization (that I missed my class), embarrassment (that I forgot), and then concern (that my dean would find out that I didn't meet my class). I didn't know what to do. So after about five minutes of thinking, I went to the dean and told on myself. That's right, I just went to her and told her what happened.

I told her that I had completely forgotten to meet my class, and that students might be contacting her about my absence. She just laughed. Then she told a story about her first year as a new professor in which she went to the wrong classroom and started passing out her syllabus to someone else's class. "No big deal. These things happen," she said.

I have thought about that day many times over the years. The first thing that pops into my head is the reason I was able to go to her. The reason that I was able to go to her and tell her this was because I trusted her. I can't really explain why I trusted her, but I did. After she told me her first-year story, I trusted her even more. She was sending the message that it's ok to mess up sometimes. I have never forgotten that message. In fact, I got the opportunity to send this message several times during my first year as a dean. I am simply paying this idea forward. It's ok to mess up. Make sure your people know that.

The Shadow CV

I am reminded of an article in *The Chronicle of Higher Education* (Looser, 2015) in which the author talked about her "shadow CV." A shadow CV is a recounting of her history of rejection as an academic. As she notes, failure is something that we, as academics, hide from people whenever humanly possible.

> That's a shame. It's important for senior scholars to communicate to those just starting out that even successful professors face considerable rejection. The sheer scope of it over the course of a career may be stunning to a newcomer. I began to think of my history of rejection as my shadow CV—the one I'd have if I'd recorded the highs and lows of my professional life, rather than its highs alone. (Looser, 2015, para. 5)

She continues to list her accomplishments (i.e., "What my CV says") and the reality of what it took to reach those accomplishments (i.e., "What my shadow CV would say"). The take away from this short article is that for every line on the CV, there are many other lines that represent the failed attempts to succeed in academe. It is refreshing to read an account of someone else's struggles to be successful in this line of work and know that we all struggle to do a good job. I would've taken solace from this article if I had read it earlier in my career. My guess is that people experience failure in different ways, and some of these feelings can be mitigated by an honest advisor or mentor during the early years of one's career. I have sent this article to my faculty in the hopes that we can begin to think of failure in the area of scholarship as part of the job. Yes, rejection as a part of the task of scholarship. But, to the new tenure track assistant professor, you wouldn't know it.

Academic CVs can be a lot like people's social media accounts. Although I deleted my Facebook account years ago (because it was interfering with my ability to focus), I remember how people took pains to put a particular spin on all their life events to give the impression that they were "winning" every day of their lives. Of course, this was all intentional. I am not the first person to point this out, or to criticize social media for these sorts of distortions (see Newport, 2016; Twenge, 2017), but social media allows us to put forth a version of ourselves that is much like a sports highlight reel. Those of you who are sports fans or who watch SportsCenter will understand the idea. The clips that make the segment are the most exciting, most impactful, most important parts of the games that they cover: the last second shot, the homerun, the touchdown catch. We do the same with our CVs, the article, the presentation, the grant, the book. We treat our CVs and the way we talk about scholarly work in the academy like people talk about their lives on social media. Our CVs are outwardly facing documents that show all of the successes without any of the hard work and rejection that comes with the territory. Our public CVs are like the carefully curated social media accounts that people use to represent themselves to the world. They represent all of the wins with none of the losses, all of the credit without any of the sweat equity, all of the successes with limited admission of the effort.

I can still remember the first article that I submitted for publication as a newly minted PhD. I submitted to a top tier journal and was predictably rejected. I can remember my university advisor giving me some guidance on the project, and even his admonitions "to not get too excited" about the article being published. "If we don't get it picked up here, we will try somewhere else," he said. When the rejection came, it wasn't a surprise. After all, as my advisor explained, publishing in academic journals is hard. Really hard. It's something that takes a lot of work and practice. The rejection that I received wasn't the part that I remember though. It was one of the rejection letters that I received. As is the standard in many fields, you have two external reviewers for your work. Two separate people read your work and give you separate, independent feedback. Usually the journal or publisher has a template that reviewers follow when they write up your strengths, weaknesses, areas for improvement, suggestions for revisions, etc. One of my reviewers sent me several pages of constructive feedback on my first attempt at publishing my work. At the time, it seemed like so much was wrong with my article, but after I thought about it for a couple days, I realized that the reviewer was right. There were some changes that needed to be made. The message was clear: Your article isn't quite ready. Make these changes. Try again.

My second reviewer wasn't so constructive. I received an email with the second review from the editor of the journal. The attachment on the email was the form review template that the first reviewer had used to write up his feedback. When I opened the attachment, I recognized the form. I was instantly drawn to the complete lack of words on the page. At the top of the first page, he included the identifying information about the journal, the title of my article, and the date. The rest of the sections remained blank. I scrolled to the second page of the review form and saw where the reviewer had made his comments. There was one sentence. It read: This is not a scholarly article. Quite an introduction to the world of academic rejection. Short and pointed—the reviewer was not a fan. I eventually reworked the article based on the comments from the first reviewer and submitted to another journal. My work was accepted for publication almost immediately. As for the second reviewer and the comments he sent, I took my adviser's advice and ignored them.

I have shared these two stories with people over the years when talking about my work. Most of the time, it is in one of those moments where we are sharing stories about how we got to where we are in academia. Or sometimes I am talking with a new faculty member about the work required to be a successful tenure track professor. I have shared the article story when I have taught seminars on academic writing. It's a good way to let the people you talk to know that you have had some failures along the way too, and that these failures are a part of what we do in academic work. What if we applied this idea to how we lead our colleges? The simple examples I have shared (missing class and getting rejected) point us to a larger idea when it comes to leadership. Although it seems counterintuitive, acknowledging weakness and failure makes you a better leader. Being vulnerable with your teams allows others to do the same, creating an environment where people aren't afraid to discuss issues openly, challenge one another, and most importantly, fail. Freed from the fear of messing up or failing, people are untethered from the arbitrary boundaries we set for ourselves. At our first faculty meeting, I gave everyone an "I blew it" certificate (Figure 9.1). This

Figure 9.1

is one of the resources from Ron Ritchhart's "Cultures of Thinking" website (http://www.ronritchhart.com/COT_Resources.html).

Although Ritchart's certificate is designed for students in a classroom setting, it fits the idea of vulnerability perfectly. This is what we see in high performing groups.

The Culture Code and the "Vulnerability Loop"

One of my favorite books that I read during my first year as dean was Daniel Coyle's *The Culture Code: The Secrets of Highly Successful Groups* (2018). In this book he writes about high performing groups. One of the findings in his book is that these groups are willing and able to be vulnerable with one another. From the leader down through the organization, people are willing to admit their mistakes, own them, and pick themselves up. He examines the Navy SEALS, Disney Pixar, and the San Antonio Spurs basketball team (among others). He is looking for the ingredients of what makes a high performing team and what leaders can do to create these conditions for their organizations. The book structured around three main skills or concepts that lead to these sorts of teams: building safety, sharing vulnerability, and establishing purpose. First, we must create an atmosphere of belonging. Coyle reports that when he was spending time with these high performing groups he would extend his research trips a day or two because he liked spending time with the people he was studying. One of the ways that we build safety within our organization is through what Coyle calls "belonging cues." How do we send the message to our people that they belong and that they are safe? The groups studied in this book did three things (Coyle, 2018, p. 11).

1. They invested energy sending the message "that people are safe here."
2. People are treated as unique and valued.
3. There is a sense that the current relationship will continue into the future.

Once people in your organization feel safe and connected to one another, they are free to focus on the important parts of the job at hand.

Second, high performing groups and their leaders exhibit a high degree of vulnerability with one another through talking about and even celebrating failures. In each of the groups that he studied Coyle noticed that they all looked at failure as a valuable part of what they did as an organization. And, the leaders were the first to go. The leaders in these groups led the way when it came to talking about struggles, failures, and then using these struggles to make the organization stronger. Being vulnerable with one another builds trust, which brings people closer together, which allows them to take more risks. This is where the loop comes in: "It builds on itself" (Coyle, 2018, p. 112). My favorite line of the book highlights the imperative for leaders to set the stage for being vulnerable, for leaders to go first and show the way.

> Normally, we think about trust and vulnerability the way we think about standing in solid ground and leaping into the unknown: first we build trust, then we leap. But science is showing us that we've got it backward. Vulnerability doesn't come after trust—it precedes it. Leaping into the unknown, when done alongside others, causes the solid ground of trust to materialize beneath our feet. (Coyle, 2018, p. 106)

Last, high performing groups are crystal clear in establishing their purpose. During the end of my first year, I thought about this idea a lot. It's the simple act of asking yourself: What is this organization about? What do we stand for? Is our purpose clear? In each of the organizations that Coyle studied, the mission of each was clear. Crystal clear. I think most often this concept is reflected in university and college mission statements, and that is where my thoughts were as I read this section of the book. A central question was at the forefront of my mind: Does the mission statement of my college reflect what we believe and does it drive what we do and the decisions we make? What are the stories that we tell about ourselves? I didn't get the impression that anyone even knew our mission statement, so the answer to these three questions was a no. As Coyle points out, mission statements and outward manifestations of an organization's purpose and mission are not simply for show. Properly conceived and utilized, these statements point people in the right direction. They can be used the same way that "... a magnetic field orients a compass needled to true north: This is why we work. Here is where you should put your energy" (Coyle, 2018, p. 187).

Make it OK for People to Follow

As we've seen from the previous section, setting the stage for leadership and positive culture is directly related to ideas about safety. A central theme is "Do your people have a sense of safety" within the culture of the group you are leading? This is the foundation on which everything else rests. This may be a shift in the way that people view leadership in your organization. The archetype of the fearless leader taking control of a situation and making bold, independent decisions isn't really the way that it works. To run complex organizations like colleges and universities, it takes more than a person who is willing to make a decision. That happens nearly every day. It is more important that we make the right decisions, and that the work of the university gets done. This is going to take more than just your courage; this takes people who are willing to follow your lead.

At one of the earliest meetings that I had with my leadership team, I introduced the idea of followership. There has been much written about this idea already so I won't recount it all here, but this idea is powerful in that it highlights the roles that followers have in being leaders. I'll say that again: it highlights the roles that followers have in being leaders. Being a good follower is a type of leadership. Followership is the reciprocal aspect of leadership. It's an examination of how well you follow a leader and how well you engage in the tasks at hand. Followership is not blind acquiescence; it is a process of helping the organization reach a legitimate goal. Some of the literature looks at typologies of people or follower "types" that we encounter as leaders. For instance, Robert Kelly (1988) lists sheep, yes people, pragmatics, alienated, and star as designations for follower types. It is a useful exercise to simply go through these descriptions with your leadership team and ask them to think about who fits into which category. For people within your college and especially people on your leadership team, they inhabit both leadership and followership spheres. They are leaders in their respective areas, but they follow you, the dean. When they go into their areas to lead, they are the leader and their people are expected to help with the work at hand, that is, follow the leader. The point of having people think about the notion of followership is not so we can convince people that they should follow us without question. It's a realization that we are all followers at some point. Deans are cast into the same situation. We are middle managers who take direction from the provost and sometimes associate provosts. We see this with department chairs, associate deans, and directors as well. One of my primary goals during my first year was communicating the idea that the people in the college were leaders, but in order to lead and get things done, we need to be good followers as well.

Metaphors and People

During my first year as a new dean, the learning curve was steep. This is expected. This came from being an outsider to the college. I had to learn people, systems, histories, and how people, systems, and histories fit together. One of the struggles that first year was not knowing what I didn't know. I would enter into conversations with faculty and staff, and before we could actually get to solving the problem or examining the issue, people would have to explain things to me. This process, although logical (i.e., asking questions before you act), is time consuming and mentally exhausting. In the early days, there was simply too much information to process in order to function. Given this fact, I did what we all do when operating in a new job—I made the best possible decision with the limited knowledge and background I had. Some days I was inundated with information about how the college worked, information that everyone else already possessed. It is almost counterintuitive to think that the person with the most power in an organization has the least knowledge about how things work. The opposite is also true. The staff who worked in the college, who had the least amount of power and authority within the college, were often the most knowledgeable about processes in the college. This fact was obvious time and time again during my early days as the dean of the college.

As the first year developed, we began to trust each other with our problems. This was perhaps the most important thing that happened with this group. It was the realization that we were in this together, and that if we discussed things, as a group, we could make things better. Over the first semester, I used several metaphors to describe what I was seeing in the college. I am a metaphor person, so I like talking using visual metaphors to make my point. Sometimes I get this right, other times I am pretty sure these only make sense in my head. But the process was always about making sense of our environment, seeing things as accurately as possible, and heading in a new direction. Metaphors allow us to describe a situation with new words, ideas, symbols, and concepts. They allow us to see common, everyday events with new eyes and with new perspectives.

Rubbing Sticks Together to Make a Fire

I often used this metaphor to describe situation in which we were, in my opinion, doing things in the college that were inefficient. The struggle with faculty on this point was that the end result was the same, so it was difficult for them to see that change was needed. Take advising as a case in point. Advising is a labor intensive, logistically complicated task that colleges perform every semester. But it needn't be. I usually used this metaphor with the chairs and/or the leadership team to emphasize that we needed to work smarter, not harder. Sometimes this could be accomplished with an adjustment to the structure of the task or by eliminating a step in the process altogether. Other times, tasks within the college could be accomplished by using readily available technologies. For example, in the college we had over 500 students turning in a form to the Office of Teacher Education every semester. We converted this form (and the physical turning it in) into an electronic form that is housed in one of the required courses in the curriculum. Around the middle of the year, I could sense that people understood that there were more efficient ways of doing things within the college. But this sense was not unanimous. It was reported to me that several people (and I am sure there were others) did not like the changes, no matter how they improved efficiency and workflow. When I was in Ohio, it was reported that one professor stated, "He acts like before he got here, that we didn't know how to do anything. It's a slap in the face to the people who worked here before he arrived." This is literally the opposite sentiment that I was shooting for, and this is the opposite sentiment that I had verbalized in meeting after meeting. We can make a fire by rubbing two sticks together, or we can use a lighter (or a torch). In both cases, we get fire. I just prefer the easier method.

Crew Team Rowing

If you are not familiar with the sport of rowing or crew, Google images or videos of this. The image of a rowing team in competition is a perfect metaphor for how I wanted our leadership team and college to operate. Rowing in the same direction, pulling their own weight, synchronized, working towards a common goal. In Patrick Lencioni's book *The Five Dysfunctions of a Team* (2002) he states this idea with clarity: "If you could get all the people in an organization rowing in the same direction, you could dominate any industry, in any market, against any competition, at any time" (p. 9). I am looking to ensure that the faculty and staff who are working in the unit are all working towards the same goals, and that we are not working at cross-purposes. You can assess how well or how poorly this happens in your college by asking people how their work fits within the work of their colleagues. Trying to establish this idea in practice is a bit more difficult than a simple conversation. I have developed, through trial and error, working at three universities a "formula" that helps people develop the mindset of "rowing in the same direction." It goes like this:

Empowerment of faculty and staff = trust =
better communication = breaking down silos

We empower faculty and staff when we allow them to make decisions within their areas of influence and expertise. We empower faculty and staff when we let them create conditions they see as beneficial for the operation of their unit or area. When you start a new deanship from the outside, you will be able to gauge by the questions that you are asked, how empowered your faculty and staff are. When faculty and staff asked me questions (oftentimes they were asking permission), I answered with another question: "What do you think?" or "How do you think we should do this?" Many times, when asked this question, the faculty or staff member didn't even realize that I was asking them their opinion because I assumed that they already knew a good way to do something. They just needed permission to do it. Empowering faculty and staff is a daily process of allowing them to make decisions about their work. In addition to discussing common issues within the college in our Dean's Council, one of the more public ways to empower faculty is to structure college wide meetings so that the faculty and staff are actually running the meeting. This begins with group planning and shared agenda creation and ends with a meeting in which more people than just the dean get to talk and guide their colleagues. This sends the message that we are moving from a culture of "me" (the dean) to "we" (the college).

This shift allows faculty and staff within the college to develop a sense of ownership over the content of the meeting, the decisions that are considered, and the overall operations of the college. Over time, framing the work of the college in this way fosters a level of trust between faculty and staff. As they see that people in the college are responsible for and answerable to each other, and that they are actually being listened to, a wonderful thing happens. People begin to trust each other, and the tenor of conversations changes. I witnessed this within my small leadership team and the larger college gatherings. I believe that the biggest barrier to doing good work is our failure to communicate with each other.

Don't misunderstand. I am not simply talking about "being nice" to one another, although that is a preferable default attitude to have with your coworkers. I am describing a relationship between faculty and staff where they respect each other so much that you feel it is your ethical obligation to tell them when they aren't doing what they should be doing. This sort of communication cuts both ways. It's between faculty, between staff, between faculty and staff, between the dean and the college, and from the college to the dean. It is best thought of as the freedom to ask questions of each other. The freedom to ask, "Why do we do it that way?" and have the person on the other end of the question respond with an attitude of gratitude that you (the questioner) want to help improve the way things are done. This requires the people being questioned to develop a sense of responsibility to the group that outweighs any sense of offense that might be taken by having your idea questioned or criticized (i.e., emotional intelligence). Just because someone questions how we are doing something does not mean that the whole thing is wrong or that it needs to be changed. That isn't the point. The point is allowing people the freedom to consider other options and ways of doing things. From this freedom comes the breaking down of silos. The irony is that these conversations about how to do things within the college rarely happen about the big things that we do.

Two good examples of this are conversations around program course-work and clinical experiences. It is arguable that these two components of colleges of education are the most important components of how we are supposed to operate. Sometimes, professors within a department are teach-ing their courses in isolation from others in the same department. This leads to, among other things, duplication of material, missing entire concepts in the curriculum, and general inefficiencies in how we teach within and across our programs. In my experience, this lack of conversation among professors in colleges of education is most prevalent around the clinical (or field) por-tion of our programs. If the coursework is the theoretical underpinnings behind teaching, the clinical portion of our programs represents the practi-cal or real-world aspects of teaching. We have our students go into real class-rooms and work with real students. Oftentimes in the field portion of edu-cation programs, the left hand doesn't know what the right hand is doing. This is a symptom of the silos that we have created in our coursework that flows down to how we think about and implement our clinical experiences. Both of these problems (i.e., silo thinking in our courses and clinical work) can be solved by allowing people to discuss what should go into a course or what clinical experiences should look like. Setting aside time in department meetings to actually map out what concepts should be housed in which courses is a very important first step to creating coherence in a department or program of study (Chapter 4). The key here is that you allow the space for faculty to work together on creating a map (or other document) that represents how the individual parts constitute the whole.

I can remember the first time that I asked my faculty, "How do we know what is being taught in which classes?" The blank stares on people's faces gave me my answer. But I asked the question again, in a different way. "Do we have a something that shows us what concepts are covered in which classes as students make their way through the program? Do we have some-thing like this that shows what our students are supposed to be doing in the field?" Faculty were in the habit of teaching their courses and assigning tasks to their students in the field, but they had overlooked the benefits of actually talking to one another, to plan and implement shared experi-ences for our students. I can remember helping the group think through this process in a college meeting and overhearing a faculty member say "So this is what shared governance looks like." Although I don't claim that what I did was the best example of shared governance, it does speak to the power of allowing faculty the space to make things better. It's actually a very common-sense approach to many of the problems we face: Empowering faculty and staff and trusting that they can solve problems, communicating a better way of doing something, and allowing them to break down silos that are counterproductive to how we conduct business. This reminds me of a quote attributed to the late Steve Jobs in which he said, "We don't hire people so we can tell them what to do. We hire people so they can tell us what to do" (Rafati, 2015). This is the basic point in empowering people. Most of the time our faculty already know that what they are doing can be done in more efficient ways. We just have to allow dialogue, clear the pathway, and get out of the way.

Physicians With Dirty Hands

This metaphor is one that I have borrowed from Simon Sinek's book, *Leaders Eat Last* (2017). This is the idea that some people in your college inflict harm on the operations of the group without realizing it. The concept that Sinek uses is that physicians in Europe during the 1700–1800s would tend to patients without washing their hands. They would visit sick and dying people, care for them, help them face the trials and tribulations of sickness and dying, while unknowingly spreading the disease themselves. Prior to germ theory and notions of modern hygiene that govern medical practice today, these caretakers of the sick and dying made things worse. They thought they were helping, but they were helping to spread disease and killing people. They weren't doing it on purpose of course, but they were responsible for the deaths of their patients in the process. We see a version of this in our organizations. There are well-intentioned people in your organization who are doing, what they feel, is the right thing. They are working hard. They care about the students and the larger mission of the college. But, they unintentionally do things that undermine the big picture. I have experience with these kinds of situations, and the response of faculty and staff to these people is almost always the same. People realize what is going on, and they say nothing. They realize that the person is well-intentioned, and they realize that the person is hurting the overall goals of the college. But no one talks to the person and tells him. No one tells the doctor to wash his hands. In these situations, we must be willing to go to the person and discuss the issue.

But what if we are the problem? In the story above, the doctors were the problem, and when people put forth the idea that they were to blame, they were ignored, or worse, attacked. Leaders can sometimes be the root problem. Yes. I am talking about you and me. As Sinek points out, we are particularly susceptible to this when we put metrics and numbers before people. Having worked at several universities, I know that this is true. We see it in the ways that we represent our work to the world and each other. It's in spreadsheets, bottom lines, and (the new fad) predictive analytics. It's in budgets, proposals for new programs, and teaching loads. I think we make a mistake when we discount one for the other, numbers for people or people for numbers. It's both. All the time. But, if we had to tip the scales to one side, it has to be tipped towards the people we lead. People come first and everything else is secondary. "All managers have an opportunity to become leaders of people . . . so too must every leader of every organization do the little things to protect their people. But first, they have to admit they are the root of the problem" (Sinek, 2017, p. 230).

Our images of leaders are that of people in front—at the front of the pack, at the start of the line. Leaders go first to show the rest of us the way. What would happen if we took this idea of being in front and going first and applied it to an examination of ourselves? And what if, along the way, we learned more about ourselves in the process? I think the answer is obvious. We'd be better leaders for it. And people would know it's safe to follow us.

References

Coyle, D. (2018). *Culture code: The secrets of highly successful groups*. New York, NY: Bantam Books.

Kelly, R.E. (1988). In praise of followers. *Harvard Business Review, 66*, 142–148.

Lencioni, P. (2002). *The five dysfunctions of a team: A leadership fable*. San Francisco, CA: Jossey-Bass.

Looser, D. (2015, October 18). Me and my shadow CV. *The Chronicle of Higher Education*. Retrieved from https://www.chronicle.com/article/MeMy-Shadow-CV/233801

Newport, C. (2016). *Deep work: Rules for focused success in a distracted world*. New York, NY: Hachette Books.

Rafati, S. (2015, June 9). What Steve Jobs taught executives about hiring. *Fortune*. Retrieved from http://fortune.com/2015/06/09/shahrzad-rafati-keeping-your-best-employees/

Richhart, R. (n.d.). *I blew it certificate*. Retrieved from http://www.ronritchhart.com/COT_Resources.html

Sinek, S. (2017). *Leaders eat last: Why some teams pull together and others don't*. New York, NY: Penguin Books.

Twenge, J. (2017). *Igen: Why today's super-connected kids are growing up less rebellious, more tolerant, less happy-and-completely unprepared for adulthood-and what that means for the rest of us*. New York, NY: Atria Books.

10

Shared Struggle

I judge you unfortunate because you have never lived through misfortune.
You have passed through life without an opponent—no one can ever know
what you are capable of, not even you.

—Seneca

BIG IDEA

BIG IDEA FOR THIS CHAPTER

As I neared the end of my first year as dean I found myself reflecting on what we had accomplished. That is the origin of this chapter: reflecting on the things we were able to do, how we were able to do them, and the people that helped along the way. Actually, "helped" is not accurate. The people that "helped along the way" were at the center of our accomplishments. They weren't tangential to our success; they were the success. After one year of serving as a college dean, I realize that I have much to learn. But there is one thing that is clear: the job of dean is about bringing the talents of the

---

group to bear on the things we need to accomplish. The things we were able to accomplish my first year are due to the collective efforts of the people in our college. What follows are my thoughts on how we were able to work together to accomplish our goals: setting norms, doing difficult things together, and adaptive leadership. I end with a note on training new deans.

This chapter is about the things we were able to accomplish during my first year as dean. The focus isn't simply on the accomplishments, but rather the ways in which we tried to set a new college culture and work with one another towards common goals. We were able to create the university's first doctoral program, create an Office of Teacher Education and Partnerships, renew our commitment to our local school partners, create several new programs, revise our internship model, launch an academic journal, create a Rural Education Center, and hire five new faculty. This is a partial list of the things we were able to do; we were able to get so much accomplished because we agreed to view the collective nature of our jobs more clearly and work towards common goals. We were able to bring our collective talents to bear on these projects and make them a reality. What follows is a brief description of how we were able to do this.

Setting Norms

The growth and development of people is the highest calling of leadership.
—Harvey Firestone

If I had to highlight the most important cultural shift we had during my first year as dean it was setting new norms for the college. I realize that this sentence sounds presumptuous. So, a caveat or two is in order. I have spent several pages of this book talking about how being the new person and not knowing things makes the job of rookie dean difficult. Yes. This is true. You may logically conclude that if you don't know things you would be unlikely able to set new norms for the people you just met. This makes sense. But that's not exactly how the year unfolded. Just because you are the new dean, and just because you don't know how everything in the college works yet, does not mean that you cannot pick up on things that need to be changed. In fact, being the new dean with new eyes allows you do to this more efficiently than people who have been in the organization for many years. Many of the things that need to be changed in your organization will be immediately clear to you because of your outside perspective. This is another reason why it is imperative to create a leadership team—so you can check your perceptions against the perceptions of the leaders in your college.

This is not to suggest that the people who were in your job before you arrived did everything wrong. In fact, they (probably) did many things well. Pointing out the things that your predecessor didn't do so well is not the point. Finding weak points in the organization and improving them is the point. This is the nature of leadership succession. People who follow a leader will change things. That's normal. People shouldn't take it personally. In fact, I hope that whoever follows me as dean of this college corrects, revises, and improves upon the things that I did as dean. That is how we will know that she is doing her job—doing the difficult things that need to be done. That is the way we should view our role and the people who follow us. Ideally, we'd like to leave the place better than we found it. We also recognize that different people bring different viewpoints and talents to the job. Having someone change the things you've done with an eye towards improvement is the way a college or university should operate. I am not offended when someone follows me and changes the things that I have done. I assume they are seeing things that I didn't see, filling in the gaps that I left behind. My only hope is that I have encouraged the organization to see change not as something to be resisted, but something to be embraced. That way the next person has an easier time implementing needed and necessary changes.

The first year is really about setting norms. To put this idea into concrete terms for the reader, I will share a few of the norms that we reset in the college. It should be noted that norms are not simply changed because the dean says they need to be changed. This, like other operations of a college, take a collective effort and buy-in from your people before they take root. When I sought to change a norm within the college I had a simple template that I followed. The purpose of this template was to get as many voices in the conversation as possible and hopefully discover possible pitfalls and obstacles before we tried to make the change. When I wanted to change a norm within the college, here are the people I consulted and the steps I followed:

1. **The Dean's Council:** The first group that I talked to about possible changes was my leadership team—the Dean's Council. This is the place where my ideas for change got their first hearing and vetting. In these meetings I told the group what I was thinking and encouraged skepticism. "Tell me why this won't work" was a line I used often. Because the people in this group represented all parts of the

college, there was always someone in these meetings that knew the potential drawbacks and pitfalls that one of my ideas would have.

2. **Chairs:** Next, I would meet with the chairs to talk about the idea again. This was usually after some time had passed from the Dean's Council meeting. This was done intentionally to allow the Chairs time to think more deeply about the idea. Sometimes we don't see problems with an idea until we think about it for a couple days. After a couple days, they were usually able to determine aspects of my idea that weren't as thought-out as I would have liked. If the chairs supported the idea, then I would ask them for time at their next department meeting to discuss the idea.

3. **Department:** After meeting with the department chairs about the proposed change, I would then visit the departmental meetings to discuss it with the faculty members. This was usually a short 10–15 minute visit with the department at the end of one of their monthly meetings. At the meeting, I would convey the message that I had an idea and that it was vetted by the Dean's Council and the department chairs. I also made it clear that the purpose of speaking to the departments was to get any feedback that they may have about the proposed change and that we would be talking about this idea again at the next full college meeting. This served not only to get feedback from the college on possible changes; it served to put the proposed changes on their radar for future consideration and discussion within the department. It also gave faculty members time to think about the change before the college met.

4. **College:** By the time the college had a chance to meet, both departments, both department chairs, and the leadership team all had a chance to think about the proposed change, provide feedback, and think about how the proposed change may impact (positively and negatively) their areas. Most of the issues that faculty had with the changes were hashed out before the college meeting, but not always. The college meeting was a public, full faculty discussion of the change. It was a chance for everyone to voice their opinion and put their objections (or support) on the table. In these meetings, I didn't do much of the talking. I usually introduced the agenda item for discussion and got out of the way. After all, I have already talked about this change already with the faculty, just in different (smaller) settings.

5. **Vote:** Lastly, the process of changing norms ended with the full college voting on these ideas. This would be done in the full faculty meeting. Full faculty votes weren't always required or even sought out, but for the changes that constituted a major shift in the way that we did things, I asked for the faculty to vote.

The simple process described above applies to the ways in which work was performed in the college. For example, when the leadership team and I decided to take a look at our professional dispositions (something that's required for our accreditation), we realized that this would be a pretty big departure from the way this had been done in the past. So, we followed the steps above. From August until April we discussed and changed the way that we performed this action in our college. This was a major change that impacted all programs and all faculty, so it took us the first two semesters to successfully make this change. For changes that fall into this category, impacting all programs and all faculty, two rules apply: get as much feedback (voice) as you can and take it slow.

There are other changes that don't require as much feedback and that can be made faster than the example I provided. These are the aspects of your college that you, as dean, need to change. These changes and the need for these changes are immediately clear to you. They don't involve the aspects of the job that are technical per se, but rather they are part of the fabric of how things are done within the college. Whereas many of the important changes that you make will be consensus-based with voices from the different areas informing your decision-making, these are more top-down shifts, cultural shifts. These changes are made through the messages that you send from the dean's office.

1. **Chain of Command:** To ensure that students and faculty are not coming to you with every issue that arises, emphasize that the dean's office is not the first place that people go when they need to complain. I made this point clear in the very first college meeting that we had in August. Faculty should go to their department chair to solve problems and resolve issues. Students should go to their professor first and then to their department chair before they make an appointment to see you. The dean's office should not be a revolving door of people making complaints. Ensure that the appropriate people are dealing with the issues in your college. When you enforce this norm, most problems are solved before they reach your office.

2. **Budgeting:** When it comes to how money is allotted and spent within the college, two words come to mind: transparency and discipline. The first year that I was dean, I made a point of sharing information with the faculty about the budget, how much money we actually had, and how it was being spent. There is no need to hide this information from people. When we do this, it gives people the impression that you are hiding something. I also instituted several basic rules around departmental budgets that helped the

chairs and their faculty to be more disciplined with their spending. I required each department to spend their own departmental travel funds before making additional requests to the dean's office. I also set an internal deadline (ahead of the end of the fiscal year) to cease spending so that we did not overspend at the end of the year. This prevented departments from trying to spend all of their money during the last days of the fiscal year. The message was clear: spend the money that you need to operate your department but be disciplined.

3. **Collective Meetings:** When the college gathered for meetings, I ensured that as many people as possible participated in the process. This actually started before the meeting was even held. For most of our monthly college meetings, I would have pre-meeting meetings with my leadership team. At these pre-meetings, we would develop the college meeting agenda. This way I ensured that the right things were being discussed and the right people were doing the talking and facilitation. Once we had developed the agenda, the meetings represented a true sharing of information. People were allowed to serve as facilitators in the meetings, sharing information, guiding the faculty, and leading their particular aspect of the college. After nearly every meeting, someone would approach me afterwards to tell me how much he/she liked our meetings. Yes. People said that they liked the meetings. That has to be a first.

4. **Sharing Information:** There are some aspects of being dean that you should not and cannot share with your faculty. This involves information of a sensitive nature, such as personnel actions or private information that faculty share with you. These are areas where discretion is key. However, most of the information that you have as dean that you use to actually run the college is not of a sensitive or personal nature. And it should be shared with your faculty. At my previous positions in higher education, this was a lesson I learned that I brought to my first dean's post. If people are getting a course release or extra money to travel, there should be an explanation that you are willing to give to people to explain your actions. Faculty may not agree with your actions, but explaining yourself is almost always preferable to hiding information from people.

5. **Gossip:** I made this very clear to my faculty early in my first year. The message was clear from the top and through the leadership team down to the units and the faculty and staff: This isn't something that we are going to tolerate anymore. Don't do it. (See Chapter 3.)

6. **Attendance at Job Talks:** I believe that getting to know potential colleagues and engaging in this process is one of the most impor-

tant things that we do as a college. Remember that interviewing and choosing our colleagues goes both ways. We are interviewing them, but they are, in a sense, interviewing us as well. We want to make a good impression on the people that we invite into our college. One way to do this is to actively participate in this process. This, of course, pertains to the search committees whose job it is to find qualified candidates, vet applications, arrange for people to come to campus, and schedule a day or so worth of activities when they come to visit us. These aspects of the job search the college seemed to do quite well. I wanted the people who were not on the search committee to take a more active role in our faculty searches when candidates came to campus. And so this was also a new norm that we set for one another. Whenever possible, I wanted our faculty and staff to meet the candidates and participate in the activities that the committee had planned. This involved attending a dinner or lunch with the candidate, driving/shuttling the candidate to the airport, and of course attending the candidates' job talks. When we had multiple searches going on simultaneously, we made sure that the schedules of the candidates included similar time slots for the candidates' job talk during a time of day convenient for faculty and staff to attend these meetings.

7. **Collegiality:** The idea of collegiality is a tricky one for some faculty. Prior to taking on the dean's position, I led efforts to create a unit-wide collegiality statement (Crookston, 2012) at a previous institution. The point of statements and documents like these are to set a group norm for what sort of behavior we expect from one another. And frankly, the overwhelming majority of faculty members exhibit what I would consider to be collegial behavior. But, there is 1–2% that don't. Statements like I am describing serve as a reminder, a collective reminder, that we have standards for how we treat one another. Another criticism of collegiality statements is that they are, in effect, attempting to control how people behave. This is not the way I intended for a collegiality statement to be perceived or utilized. Having the faculty agree to a statement or collection of statements about shared norms about behavior is a good thing. It sets the stage for how we see one another and how we treat one another in our daily work. This is something I plan to do in my second year as dean.

8. **Personal Mantra:** During the second semester, I was talking with a trusted colleague from another institution about being dean and the shift in thinking that occurs when you move to the dean's chair. And she asked something that made me think. She asked, "Do your people know what you are about?" I told her that I had laid out my

personal ideas about leadership in my introductory remarks to the college when the year started. But she wasn't talking about what I said in a meeting. "Do they know what you are about? If someone outside of the college asked about the new dean, what would people say?" She suggested that I start telling people what I was about—on a regular basis. This concept is also included in Coyle's (2018) book, *The Culture Code*. High performing groups have collective mantras that they all are able to recite and talk about. It describes how the organization operates and what values are most important. The more I thought about this, I realized that we did (collectively) have a mantra. I had been discussing these ideas with faculty and especially the leadership team all year long. Only I hadn't put something down on paper. When people ask about the new dean in the college of education and what we, as a college are about, I want people to know three phrases:

Work Hard.

Be Kind.

Own It.

We work hard, we are kind to one another, and we take ownership for the work in our college.

To have a successful college of education it takes a ton of hard work by many people working in concert. Given the state of funding to higher education, we are doing more with less. We are required to do more than was required in the past, oftentimes with fewer resources. And this is just the operational side of the college. I am not even talking about the typical aspects of university work (teaching, scholarship, and service). In our college, we work hard to accomplish our collective goals.

We are kind to one another because it sets the stage for great things to happen. This is the collegiality piece of the equation. Our college is a small group of 25–30 full-time faculty and staff. Having collegiality and kindness as a shared, expected norm allows us to do good work that we are here to do. Toxic, harmful, non-collegial environments prevent us from doing this work. If people ask about our college, I'd like for people to know that we are kind to one another, and that this is a shared expectation that we have of the people we invite into our tribe.

Last, I'd like for people to know that we, as a college, own our destiny. Yes, this sounds a bit dramatic. I am ok with that. I want people to feel empowered enough to own their programs, their departments, their problems, and their successes. You know this idea has taken root if people don't look to others to solve their problems. If you ask faculty members about an issue or problem you will see this very clearly. Your answer is immediately clear in the way that the group responds to your question. You ask a question about a perceived problem that needs to be fixed. What do people do? I mean, what is their actual, physical response? There are usually two typical responses: people shrug their shoulders and look around at the other people in the meeting to see who is to blame, or people raise their hands and say, "That's my area. I will take care of this problem." Own it is found in the latter response. This outlook on the work of a college has a ripple effect that goes across the entire organization. When one person or one area begins to feel ownership over their area, others take notice and do the same. The way that the college operates looks, sounds, and feels different because this idea is contagious. It just takes a couple of people (or leaders) to go first to tap into the interconnectedness of the work that takes place in your college. I have worked in organizations in which the faculty and staff's default response to problems was to look to the top. It was almost as if the group was helpless (they weren't, it just felt that way) without the leader to tell them what to do. I prefer the opposite. I prefer that the people in the organization take ownership of their problems and actively seek out solutions. I prefer helpful to helpless.

I discussed this three-line mantra with faculty in subtle and not so subtle ways during my first year. I was also fortunate enough to interview several candidates for positions in our college, and when they would ask about the college, I would integrate this into my answer. More than one of the candidates asked me a very pointed question: "What are you looking for in this job?" There is a technical answer to this question that can mostly be found in the job advertisement. We are looking for a person with these experiences, this degree, these sorts of publications, experience with public schools, etc. That's the technical answer. Then there is the culture answer. "What are you looking for?" actually has to be reframed. It's not what am I looking for. It's better thought of as, "What are we looking for?" Our college is looking for someone who works hard, is kind to the people they work with, and who owns it. I assume that the candidates we hire are smart and qualified. Otherwise, they wouldn't be in the interview. In my mind, those aspects are given. Yes, some people are more qualified than others and this is clear by looking at their CVs and other materials. I am less concerned with what you have done, and more concerned with what you can help us accomplish moving forward. This is what I told our candidates. I think it is fair to be completely upfront with people who want to join our college. This is what we are about. Advice that I got many years ago fits into this conversation. That advice is to go ahead and tell people who you are and what you are about. Be explicit about what you and the organization need. People are going to make up a narrative about you anyway, so it might as well be informed with aspects that represent what you believe. I have found that the things people make up about you is never as good as the truth, so go ahead and tell people. Tell people who you are. Often.

Running 40s

I have already shared with you that I used to be a middle school football coach. And, although it may seem weird to talk about coaching 7–8th graders in a book about being a new dean, I think the connections to leading a sports team and leading a college are very similar. The school where I coached was a small K–12 school in northern Alabama with a history of losing seasons. When I took over the job of coaching this team we had less than 20 players. We had fewer people on our roster than just about anyone we played that year. I can remember when our practices started in late August, I didn't know how we'd compete with teams with deeper rosters. The only way to compete with these other teams was to make sure that we were in better shape than our opponents. So that's what we did. We got in shape. It is customary for football practices to end with the entire team running 40-yard sprints, colloquially called "40s." The concept is simple. You run 40 yards as fast as you can to get your body used to quick bursts of running that is required in the game of football. Once you run 40 yards, the coach waits 10–20 seconds, and blows the whistle. Off you go in the other direction, sprinting 40 yards again. It's hard. It's painful. And, if done with effort, it makes you a better team. This exercise and the collective nature of it—the shared experience of running with your teammates, the shared pain of struggling to catch your breath in the Alabama heat and humidity, serves to bond players together.

Most of the time, high school and middle school football practices end with players running 10–15 40s. This is a typical amount of running that is done at the end of practices to ensure that the team is in good enough shape to play the game. Of course, we didn't have many players, so it was imperative that we were in better shape than most of the teams we'd be playing. Each practice I would add to the number of 40s that we'd run after practice. At first players protested. Eventually, it became a part of the way we ended our practices. Then something happened with the team and the way they viewed running 40s. It became a shared expectation for the team. I reiterated to them that we'd have to be in better shape than the people we played, or we couldn't compete. Their players would be able to take breaks during the game. We wouldn't. So, we better be able to run all game long. Eventually, our practices ended with 20 40s, then 50, and by the middle of the 3rd week or so, 100. Yes. One hundred 40s. I can still remember the head coach of the varsity team asking me what I was doing. I just told him that we were getting ready for our next game. Which we won handily. In fact, in two years, we lost twice. We beat teams that were stronger and faster and who had more players. But we were built to last the entire game, and so we usually pulled away in the 4th quarter. Their players were exhausted. Our players looked like they did in the 1st quarter.

Something else happened with our team that's worth noting. During the time in which I was increasing the amount of running that we were doing, I had a player lash out at me during practice one day. We were running 40s, and he was tired. That much running is hard. It's painful, and it seems like it's never going to end. In his frustration at me blowing my whistle, he yelled at me. I was doing my best to encourage them to keep at it, to push through, to stick together and encourage one another. For most of the players, this worked. You could see them encouraging each other to push through. I even had some players run down and push their teammates across the finish line. But not this guy.

"Come on guys. This is where we become a team. Where we win our games. We win before we even take the field. We've got to be in better shape than the guy across from us . . ."

At this point, the player exploded. He barked at me to run like they were having to do. In fact, he was challenging me. The message was clear. Here we are working our butts off while you just stand there and blow your whistle. This is harder than you think. Why don't you get out here and do it? So I did. From that point on, I ran 40s at the end of practice with my players. I took on the role of coach and encourager. And, he was right. It was hard, and it was painful. And, we were going to do this together. Yes, we managed to win most of our games, and we managed to do so (most of the time) in convincing fashion, but that's not the point of this story. The point of this story is that our team was made stronger by the collective struggle that we endured at the end of each practice. Those experiences are what made our team a team, coach and all. The culture of our team was forged in the struggle of running 40s. More than winning or playing the game well, our culture was built in those moments of effort on late summer afternoons at the end of practices.

Two lessons from those humid Alabama afternoons inform how I see my role as dean. First, never ask your people to do something you aren't willing to do yourself. I realize that this is probably off-putting to many readers. Comparing an eighth grade boy complaining during football practice to leading faculty and staff at a university seems absurd. Only, it's not. That player, in that moment, became one of the leaders of my team. From that point forward, he became one of the reasons that we were a winning team. He wasn't trying to challenge my authority or disrespect me. He was telling me how he felt in that moment. I think leaders everywhere would do themselves a favor if they listened to the voices of everyone in their organization, not just the people who tell them things they want to hear. Secondly, your relationship with your leadership team is solidified in the crucible of collective struggle. Again, I know that there are readers who will scoff at the idea that the work of faculty and staff in a university setting is akin to football players running sprints to get in shape. I disagree. They are more alike than I think we want to believe. Many of the things we do in colleges and universities constitute very difficult work. With decreasing funding and resources to accomplish the jobs we are hired to do, we must work together. We are called to: create new programs, increase enrollment, earn accreditation, be excellent teachers, produce quality research, work with local school partners, increase external funding—at the same time. To many university faculty, these goals sound impossible. To my middle school football players, running 100 40s and actually winning games sounded impossible too. The power of shared suffering and struggle binds people together.

This is the experience that I had during my first year as a dean with my leadership team. I was witness to the power of shared, collective struggle and learning to work towards common goals. Relationships and leadership acumen was created and formed in moments of collective struggle towards common ends.

Birds in Formation

When I was a boy, I would go fishing in a creek near my house. In the summertime, that was my favorite thing to do. I'd gather up my tackle box and fishing rod, hop on my bike and ride the three or four miles to the creek. Once there, I'd spend most of the day fishing and exploring the woods. In the fall, when the leaves began to change, I can remember watching ducks flying south in formation. This was my cue that fishing was getting close to being over for the year. The weather would turn colder and the days of wading in the creek and fishing would be over until the next spring. I have often thought of the birds flying south in formation as a metaphor for leadership. When I was in middle school, I checked out a book from our school library that included a description of the V shaped pattern that ducks and geese use to make the trek to warmer weather for the winter. The term for this is skein (pronounced |'skān|). The book talked about how people throughout history wondered why birds flew in this distinctive pattern during the fall months. There were two main pre-scientific theories to explain this phenomenon. First, people thought that they took this pattern because the birds were simply following the leader. This makes sense. The birds were simply following the dominant or alpha member of the flock. Another theory was that by flying in this pattern it somehow made the journey easier for the birds. It turns out that they were both correct. The birds are simply following the leader and flying in this pattern does make the journey easier. The birds, in effect, take turns being the leader, taking on the wind and the friction away from the birds that follow, making the journey easier on the ones that follow. That is until they get exhausted by the work. When this happens, the lead bird falls back to the rear of the formation, and another leader steps up to take on the challenge and work of leading the group. This pattern of leading the group, taking turns, and getting to their destination is a collective effort. It's not accomplished by one bird leading the way for the entire journey. It's not accomplished by the rest of the group sitting back and allowing one or two members of the team do all of the work while they coast on the efforts of the few. The destination is made possible by the realization that they are stronger together, that everyone has a role to play, and if we get to where we want to go, it will be because of our ability to lead when it's our turn and follow when it's someone else's turn. This is the power of a good leadership team. This is what I experienced during my first year as a dean. When the work and the struggle became too much for one person to shoulder, another member of the team would assume the lead position and lead the group.

The difficulty and struggles of being a new dean are hard on you, but it also stresses the systems and the people that were in place when you arrived. This means that the struggle is not yours alone to bear. Others will have to do things in a different way, see problems through different lenses, and learn how to work within new systems. Some of this new learning is technical, but most of this shift for you and your people is in the way you/we view our work in relation to others. This shift is not so much individual, but relational. How does your work and your skills and talents fit with the work, skills, and talents of others? By the end of the year, the pieces of our leadership puzzle began to come into focus, with the outlines of our work becoming more visible. The point here is that for the internal struggles that you face as a new dean, the people within your leadership team face similar struggles and adjustments as well. They are on this journey with you. You are not alone. They are learning and adjusting too. We are all better off when we recognize that this collective adjustment is taking place and is a part of the leadership journey. Struggles that we faced together our first year included:

■ **Doing Things That Had Never Been Done by the College:** During the first year, members of the leadership team helped guide our college towards the first doctoral degree in the history of the university (EdD in Educational Leadership). Also, we were able to improve our relationship with the local schools after years of a strained atmosphere. These are two of the accomplishments that we made the first year that truly represent uncharted territory for our college. Anytime you attempt something new, there is an opportunity to grow and evolve. In the first year, there were plenty of opportunities.

▪ **Facing the Past:** For some on the leadership team, my short time as dean allowed a sort of reset for thinking about their work and place in the college. The truth was that not everyone enjoyed his or her role/place within the college structure. There were many reasons for this including past leadership styles, personal disagreements, and a negative working environment. During my first month on the job, I met with every faculty and staff in the college to get to know them. It was in these meetings that this discomfort/tension with the pre-existing would come out. The same was said for people on the leadership team. It seemed to be a cathartic moment to say things that needed to be said, to name the aspects of working in the college that they thought didn't work or that were harmful to people. For the entire first year, there seemed to be a constant checking and rechecking to see if the things we were doing fit with the past. I don't think it was intentional. I think it was a natural reflex to doing things a certain way and working within a particular environment. This shift was a departure from the past, and this took some adjustment.

▪ **Learning Things We Should Already Know:** Just because I created a formal leadership team within the college, it didn't mean everyone was completely prepared to take on the issues and problems that we faced. In fact, the people that made up the leadership team didn't know how to do many of the things that they were called on to do. For all of their help during the first year, there were times when I would ask a member of the leadership team a question, and they simply wouldn't know. I can remember thinking (and sometimes saying out loud): "But you are supposed to know how to do this." Maybe they were supposed to know, but they didn't. That's okay too. We learned to accept this fact and moved towards learning together. It was in these moments that I would remind myself that the way this leadership team was operating and working within the college was a new thing. New requires that we learn how. They'd never had a leadership team, so of course there'd be gaps in their knowledge and skill base. The basic outline of our collective learning was: ask a question— realize we don't know—discuss—figure it out together. This way of doing things was oftentimes frustratingly slow. We'd spend our time figuring out things that we should, or somebody should, already know. But, in the process of struggling to figure it out, we became stronger as a unit.

▪ **Reframing the Way We See our Colleagues and Taking on New Challenges:** For the members of the leadership team, collective leadership was new. This isn't to say that they were not leaders before I arrived, because they were. They just didn't know it. Their definition of leadership needed to be expanded. Leadership to them was a matter of getting permission to be great, instead of going ahead and being great. With these shifts in mindset, everyone was doing things they'd never done before. Everyone on the leadership team was not only doing more, they were being asked to use this same concept (empowering others to lead) with the people in their areas.

▪ **Learning How to Let Go:** A major part of the idea of empowering others is being able to let go and not control everything. This is harder for some than others. This requires a degree of patience to allow others to find solutions to problems instead of finding a solution for them. If we are to instill leadership in others, we must be willing to extend the same space to them to figure things out that we'd like extended to us.

New Dean Training

The audience for this book is really anyone interested in leadership at the dean level in a college or university. This would include rookie deans, department chairs who want to be a dean someday, and other administrators (associate deans, etc.) who currently support the work of a college dean. This final section of this chapter deals with processes and endings. I am speaking of processes as the things that we collectively do to get work accomplished. This refers simply to how we do things in our colleges. In fact, most of what I have written about in this book can be categorized as the way we do things around here. Navigating the process and bringing people along with you is a major part of the way I view college leadership. That much we have covered. The other part of this section deals with endings. For those of us who work in higher education, we have endings each semester and year. These arbitrary demarcations of time serve to remind us that a time period is over and that another one is about to begin. I have always enjoyed the fact that we have three beginnings and endings in our work year: fall semester, spring semester, summer semester. With each start and finish, we have an opportunity to reflect and try and improve on what we did before. Our jobs don't stretch into the future in perpetuity. Our time is segmented with opportunities to change, redirect, reflect, and improve. The metaphor of the chalkboard (or whiteboard) is apt. At the end of a class or lesson, the teacher erases the material from the board to start anew when the class meets again. I believe that leadership can follow this same idea. To start anew with fresh ideas and try again.

In my career, I have experienced this before. I have ended a semester and taken the time before the next to rethink and revise how I do things. After working in higher education for over a decade, I have made strides in being a better professor and leader, but the process is ongoing. And for this new chapter in my life, it has, more than any other year, required that I work with others to accomplish my goals. This is where gratitude comes in. During the last Dean's Council meeting of the year, I gave these certificates to the team (See Figure 10.1 and 10.2).

CERTIFICATE *of* ACHIEVEMENT

THIS ACKNOWLEDGES THAT

Name Here

HAS SUCCESSFULLY COMPLETED THE

Rookie Dean Training Program

For meritorious service, extreme patience, and courage in helping to lead the College (while working with a new dean). I am eternally grateful, and the College is stronger because of your efforts. Thank you.

2017-18
ACADEMIC
YEAR

PRENTICE T. CHANDLER, DEAN
COLLEGE OF EDUCATION

Figure 10.1

Figure 10.2 Dean's Council 2017–2018. Back Row: John McConnell (Associate Dean), Lisa Barron (Director of Teacher Education and Partnerships), Jana Hatcher (Coordinator of Certification and Licensure). Front Row: Theresa Dezellem (Academic Associate to the Dean), Moniqueka Gold (Department Chair), Prentice Chandler (Dean), Benita Bruster (Department Chair)

The wording of the certificate was a bit tongue in cheek, but it also represented my thoughts and feelings about the gratitude I had for their support during the first year. I actually thought about calling it the "Rookie Dean Training Simulator," but as a friend rightly pointed out, they didn't experience a simulation—they experienced the real thing. Yes, they did.

The leadership team experienced all of the ups and downs and the triumphs and failures of my first year with me. It is because of their support and leadership that they were able to accomplish great things and we, together, have made our college stronger.

We have the right people in the right places and that has made all the difference. I am fortunate to be surrounded by leaders who have been patient and gracious with me as I learned the ropes during my first year as dean.

References

Coyle, D. (2018). *The culture code: The secret of highly successful groups.* New York, NY: Bantam Books.

Crookston, K. (2012). *Working with problem faculty: A six-step guide for department chairs.* San Francisco, CA: Jossey-Bass.

11

The Inner Landscape of Leadership

The growth and development of people is the highest calling of leadership.

—Harvey Firestone

BIG IDEA FOR THIS CHAPTER

During my first year, I tried to steer the leadership team and the college towards notions of adaptive leadership (Heifetz, 1994). If you will recall from Chapter 2, the basic premise behind this idea is that there are three main ways that we can approach a problem:

BIG IDEA

1. Apply a solution that you've used in the past that fixes the problem.
2. Apply a solution that you've used in the past that doesn't quite fit and may make the problem worse.
3. Recognize that old solutions won't work with this new problem and learn/adapt to solve it.

In this final chapter, I provide some thoughts on how to implement this idea. In *Leadership Without Easy Answers* (1994), Heifetz offers an outline of ideas to help leaders manage themselves. He provides us with "seven practical suggestions for bearing the responsibility that comes with leadership without losing one's effectiveness or collapsing under the strain" (p. 252). His list of seven suggestions forms the outline for this chapter.

There is a paradox inherent in the daily existence of a leader. You are surrounded by people all day long, you are constantly talking with and responding to people, and people are in and out of your office. During my first year as dean, my calendar was full of events to attend, groups of people to meet with, and opportunities for speaking engagements. I worked with many different people in many different settings nearly every day. I had a great leadership team that I relied on for advice and counsel, and I was constantly walking the halls of our college trying to meet students and chat with faculty. The paradox inherent in all of this is that being a dean and the leadership responsibilities that are foisted upon you can create a solitary existence. You are at once the center of the storm and somehow disconnected from it completely. The role causes a sense of loneliness that, in light of the many people you work with and the variety of functions that you attend, doesn't seem to make much sense. I believe that these feelings are lessened by creating a leadership team and leaning on others for guidance, but the feeling is still there. As I have said many times throughout this book, my conception of leadership involves many people striving towards common goals, so I know I am not alone in this job, it just feels that way sometimes. As leaders we are caught in the nexus of people, their dreams and goals, and some future version of the world. No matter the advice you glean from your team and no matter how much you think and rethink decisions, they are, at the end of the day, your decisions. This is where solitude enters the room, and where I have found some of the most difficult parts about being a dean.

I have come to realize what I am sure seasoned deans already know: managing your inner landscape (Palmer, 2017) is a major part of being able to lead others. It sounds sort of trite to say, but leading and/or managing others is impossible if we can't lead/manage ourselves. Heifetz's list helps us think about how we might do this. In the pages that follow, I take Heifetz's suggestions and talk about how I managed myself so that I might lead others. Sometimes I was successful in these attempts, and other times I wasn't. But the point is that we as leaders spend time and effort thinking about how we see ourselves in the leadership process. As leaders we are so used to making judgments and analyses about things that are external to us. But, what if we turned the judgments inward? What do we see, feel, and sense when we turn the lens on ourselves? Heifetz suggests that we:

1. Get on the balcony
2. distinguish self from role,
3. externalize the conflict,
4. use partners,
5. listen, using oneself as data,
6. find a sanctuary, and
7. preserve a sense of purpose (p. 252).

Get on the Balcony

The metaphor of "getting on the balcony" is useful in thinking about how to navigate the landscape of leadership. Heifetz (1994) describes this as:

> the experience of dancing on a dance floor in contrast to standing on a balcony and watching other people dance. Engaged in the dance, it is nearly impossible to get a sense of the patterns made by everyone on the floor...To discern the larger patterns on the floor—to see who is dancing with whom, in what groups, in what location, and who is sitting out which kind of dance—we have to stop moving and get to the balcony. (pp. 252–253)

In order to experience the dance as well as perceive the patterns and big picture of the dance requires a framework for thinking about how we lead, the people we lead, and the decisions we must make. This includes, "identifying the adaptive challenge, regulating distress, directing disciplined attention to the issues, and giving the work back to the people" (Heifetz, 1994, p. 254).

Identifying the Adaptive Challenge

One problem that we faced early in my time as dean involved two interrelated aspects of the work that we do in colleges of education. This included revising the way that our students worked in schools (as a part of their program) and improving our relationship with the local schools. I have touched on these already, but this represents a classic case of adaptive leadership. Both represented problems for which old solutions and ways of thinking would not work. Although the phrase "think outside the box" is worn out, that is what we were forced to do—to think of new solutions to old problems and work together to learn how this might unfold.

For us this challenge was structural and personal. Structurally, we had to rethink why this aspect of our program looked the way that it did. Next, we had to explore whether or not this was the best way to do it or if we were doing it this way out of tradition. Once it was decided that we were doing things because that's the way we'd always done it the path opened up for changes. Our thinking on these issues began to evolve. We reduced the number of intern sites, decreased the number of placements, discussed and mapped course requirements, negotiated field work goals and objectives, and made this aspect of our programs more intentional. These changes ensured that we were doing things for the right reasons with the right people in the right places. Tradition no longer was the driving force behind why we did things. Is there a better way to do this? There is? Ok. Let's do it that way.

The personal aspect of this challenge revolved around improving our relationship with the local schools. Admittedly, this challenge was more complex than the structural issues I describe above. The reasons for this are simple. Attitudes and culture are harder to change than structures. I believe that there were two decisions about mindset that made all the difference about this adaptive challenge. First, we made a conscious decision to talk less and listen more. People who work in public schools have one of the hardest jobs in the world. Is our relationship with them making their job harder or easier? Are we helping or hurting their efforts? Do they see us as equal partners or do they feel that we are ignoring their needs? Do they see us as a valuable part of what they do or not? The only way to determine the answers to these questions and to form a true, proactive partnership is to talk less and listen more. After all, we want the same things. Our college of education and the local school district both want good teachers and educated children. We were on the same team. We just didn't know it.

The second shift we decided to make was to frame our work as collaborative. From our very first meetings with the local schools to talk about our partnerships, I laid out our vision of why these meetings and connections were important. Stated plainly, it is the responsibility of colleges of education and the local school districts to prepare good teachers. The emphasis in that last sentence is on the word and. Early in our conversations with our partner district, I was impressed by all of the things they are already doing to support and improve the teachers they employed. I knew the great work that professors in colleges of education did, but it was always framed as separate and in isolation from the efforts of schools once our graduates were hired. We were doing great things in the college. They were doing great things in the district. We simply weren't talking to one another. If it were simply lack of communication between us, that would be one thing. It's not just that we weren't communicating—that would almost be a neutral sounding result. But, it was worse than that. The result of this was not neutral. It was a net negative for the thing that we both claimed to be about—educating children. When we don't work together in a true partnership, we are negating the potential to make our educational system, the academy and the public schools, better.

Regulating Distress

Part of our work involved regulating the distress that is part of any major change. The disequilibrium that followed our meetings and discussions about revising our partnership with the district consumed a lot of mental energy for the people working on this project. The reason for this is simple. What we, in colleges of education, do in the field is a major part of our identity as a college. For students majoring in education, studying to be teachers, the field experience component of their time at a university is, arguably, the most important part of their degree. Studying education at a university exemplifies a melding of theoretical and practical considerations about the profession of teaching, with student teaching representing the capstone experience for our students. Revising the way that we did field experiences and student teaching within the college, across all programs, was a significant undertaking involving every program and every faculty member in those programs.

Additionally, the stakes are high for colleges of education in the state of Tennessee. Every state has its own way of monitoring the progress of teacher education programs in their state. The state of Tennessee produces an annual state report card that highlights the strengths and weaknesses of its graduates. Much of what gets reported in these data is connected to the work that our students do once they are hired as a teacher. The pressure for our students to perform well as teachers and its connection to the internship that they do at the end of their program added to our stress during this process. We have to get it right.

How did we regulate the distress of our faculty and our partners in the schools? The first aspect that we highlighted was that this process would take at least one academic year. In this way we highlighted the process over the end product. Yes. We would be making some drastic changes to the way we do our internship, but it will take us some time to discuss, revise, and change. This allowed everyone time to adjust to the changes that we were making. It also allowed us time to build a real relationship with the school district, instead of just having a meeting to tell them what we were doing. Second, we made changes throughout the college that supported our partnership changes, so that changes were part of a larger project to streamline and connect different aspects of our programs. Lastly, we had regular meetings in which we solicited feedback and communication from our partners. Monthly luncheon meetings were perhaps the most important distress regulator that we had in this process. Sitting down, having a good lunch, and discussing common problems that we were having went a long way towards solidifying our partnership with the schools. One meeting in particular highlights this idea. As I have said before, partnerships between colleges of education and school districts can make or break efforts to educate the next generation of teachers. It is hard to overestimate the importance of these relationships. We have mandates and considerations that are not always perfectly aligned with the mandates and considerations of the local schools. Sometimes, this makes for a difficult task. We knew this. The school district knew this. So, this is a fact that we acknowledged when we came to our meetings. But this wasn't the whole picture. The state department of education was also a major player in this equation. Their absence at our meetings was highlighted by one of the leaders from the school district. The body that sets and enforces policy for the public schools and colleges of education wasn't at the table. So, we invited them. Inviting all three parties to our meetings was a first for our college. It also served to alleviate some of the stress that comes with doing this sort of work. It allowed each party to see the issues and dilemmas that the others faced in doing this work. Since the college, the school district, and the state had different stressors, this was the first time that we all got to talk about specific challenges and how we might help each other in the process.

Directing Disciplined Attention to the Issues

Revising our internship structure and improving our relationship with the district required discipline. The good news for us in the college and the leaders at the district level was that each organization had new leadership. We were able to start fresh. Our college had a new dean, and the district had a new director. Additionally, this sort of work was already ripe for us to address because part of the process was directed by the state department of education. They were requiring that colleges of education and local school districts develop what they called "primary partnerships" with one another. Schools and colleges had always had relationships with one another, but this was different. It was a more formalized agreement that required true partnership work take place. The time was right.

Although this was a new expectation from the state, how we made this happen was up to the college and the district. This is where everyone involved recognized that this was a great opportunity to hit reset. In our college we felt that the time was right to rethink not only what we did in the college relative to internship, we felt it was necessary to rethink how we viewed our partners in the schools. We knew that it was counterproductive to work against one another. Only by collaborating and working towards common ends would we be successful in this effort.

Giving the Work Back to the People

This aspect of adaptive leadership, as it pertains to this project, is a theme that has run throughout this book. What we were able to change and accomplish with our partners was the result of having many voices at the table and listening to those voices. It required a shift in thinking of our partners from simply as a place where we could send our student teachers to seeing them as an integral part of educating teachers. But it didn't just stop there. The other shift that we made was to give this work to the people. Instead of the dean of the college and the director of schools getting together and figuring all of this out, the planning, ideas, and implementation was done by the faculty and leadership of each organization. The people in each organization took ownership of this process from the very beginning. It was clear that this was something that we would need to do as a team or it wasn't going to work. There were simply too many considerations, too much to change, and too many moving parts for this to be the work of one person at our college. The department chairs, the director of teacher education, and our faculty worked all year long to make changes to the way we did things in the college to support this partnered effort.

Distinguish Self From Role

> A person who leads must interpret people's responses to his actions as responses to the role he plans and the perspective he represents. (Heifetz, 1994, p. 263)

There is a tendency to take everything personally when you are the leader of a group. People's response to you is more about the role that you play than you personally. This is informed by the history and context of the institution and the faculty's relationship with the previous leader. Do what you think is right, go through appropriate and established routes to get things done. Be ethical and fair. Make decisions. The rest is noise. Are people responding to you, as a person, or are they responding to the role that you play as the dean? There is a balancing act that I struggled with during my first year. This act is represented by getting information and feedback from your faculty and staff about an issue in order to make a decision on the one hand, while having the sole authority (for most issues) to make a decision on the other. There is a recognition that you must rely on others' opinions to make decisions, but that you must remain independent in the decisions that you are forced to make. Although the following quote is not an exact fit for being a dean, it does hit on the spirit of what I am trying to describe. It's from James Comey's (2018) book *A Higher Loyalty: Truth, Lies, and Leadership*. For me it's important to maintain this idea in the face of difficult decisions, that you try to do the right thing rather than the political or popular thing.

> I don't care about politics. I don't care about expediency. I don't care about friendship. I care about doing the right thing. And, I would never be part of something I believe to be fundamentally wrong. I mean, obviously we make policy judgments where people disagree, but I will do the right thing. (p. 94)

Externalize the Conflict

> Internalizing the conflict causes serious difficulties... The issue readily becomes personalized and gets interpreted as a personal problem even when it is not. Furthermore, it produces work avoidance because it allows people to deflect their attention from the issue to the person, and to shift responsibility to him. (Heifetz, 1994, p. 266)

When there is conflict, do we internalize or externalize the conflict? If we internalize it, we are making a choice to shoulder the burden of solving it by ourselves. If we externalize the problem and the conflict that follows, we are "giving the conflict back to its rightful owners" (Heifetz, 1994, p. 264). One of the things that I tried to do during the first year was to frame problems or issues in terms of who they belonged to. I know this is a strange way to think of problems, especially for people who are in positions of leadership. In a way, all problems that we face belong to everyone. But, that is too broad to be operational. On the other end of the spectrum are leaders who view problems (and their resolutions) as the responsibility of the leaders. Perhaps you have worked with leaders like this. They are the ones who try and solve every problem, for every person, every day. I tried to find a middle ground when it came to addressing and hopefully solving problems. I would routinely ask, "What are we talking about here? What is the actual problem and who does it belong to?" In asking these questions, I was trying to guide people to the root of an issue—the actual problem. This may sound reductionist, but I have found that many times we don't actually focus on the root problems, instead focusing on tangential aspects of a problem. When we do this, we address aspects of the problem, instead of the problem. In the end, we are left with a slightly better version of the same problem, instead of a solution.

_____

Use Partners

> Even if the weight of carrying people's hopes and pains may fall mainly, for a time, on one person's shoulders, leadership cannot be exercised alone. (Heifetz, 1994, p. 268)

As I have shown, leadership is not a solo activity. If you have made it this far, you know that this is a theme throughout this book. I think of this concept in two categories. The first is working with a group of people who you rely on. The second is more personal and involves individual people that you trust to help you make decisions. Both types require that you be comfortable asking questions, that you check your perceptions against the perceptions of others, and that you develop a tolerance for ambiguity. This is how many of our meetings would unfold. Instead of issuing directives and giving orders to the people on the team, the meeting was punctuated by questioning an idea, looking for weak points, and trying to (as a group) develop the best course of action going forward. This idea applied to our big picture planning as well as when we would plan college-wide meetings. My default position is that we can develop a better course of action than I could by myself. Yes, it takes more time and patience to do it this way. Yes, it seems more efficient and easier to just do it yourself. But, we almost always trumps me. Two heads or three heads or seven heads are usually better than one.

The other way that I used partners can be divided into what Heifetz (1994) called confidants and allies. The confidant is the person that you vent to at the end of the day who can provide context and perspective for the issues you are struggling with. They direct us by asking: What is really happening? What is causing the problem? What is the next move? What mistake did we make? What does this mean (Heifetz, 1994)? I have confidants on the leadership team as well as confidants who are external to the university. These people are integral to your survival as a new dean. These people provide a special service to us who work in leadership. They provide a sounding board for our ideas (good and bad), help us to process the ups and downs of the job, and help us to make sense of what is happening around us. In a way they serve as our compass or GPS. They listen, assist, and help to get us facing in the right direction again. My confidants help me to process, serve as a release valve (for the tough days), and tell me when I am wrong or headed down the wrong path. Help to process things, release valve, tell us when we are wrong. These people have been invaluable to me in my first year as a dean.

An ally is a "partner usually operating across a line of authority or organizational boundary...will share a value or point of view and will often confide in each other about specific strategic questions..." (Heifetz, 1994, p. 268). For me, this referred to my relationship with other deans across campus. I was not able to form strong relationships with this group during my first year. With so much to learn and do during the first year, I mostly focused inward, to issues in my college. We discussed issues, met regularly, and I, of course, had questions, but these relationships took a back seat to the work I was doing in my college and the leadership team and culture I was building in my college. Having said that, there were deans who were instrumental in helping our college to achieve its goals. The dean of the graduate college was very involved in helping us to secure our first doctoral degree, and the dean of the college of STEM was active and helpful in our collaborations around science education and outreach. I also realized during the first year that deans of the other colleges were more than willing to collaborate on projects and across disciplinary lines, which is great news for any dean. I look forward to working more closely with them in the future.

Listening, Using Oneself as Data

> To interpret events, a person who leads needs to understand his own ways of processing and distorting what he hears. To sustain the stresses of leadership, he needs to know enough about his own biases to compensate for them. (Heifetz, 1994, p. 271)

People who attempt to lead an organization rely on their perceptions to make judgments and decisions. This makes sense. This is how we operate as we go through life. Our senses give us perceptions that we then act on to navigate the world. But, when you are new leader in a new environment, your perception isn't always accurate. By the very fact of your newness, your perception on some things is probably wrong. Let that last sentence sink in: when you are new, your perception on some things is probably wrong. So, this part of your job, the part where you try to perceive and interpret a new environment so that you can make appropriate decisions, is hard. And, you need help. Your interpretation of the landscape is always partial. It is partial in at least two ways: It is partial because it is always incomplete, and it is partial because it is always based on your subjective understandings. Even when you try to collect all of the information about something and attempt to hear all sides, objectivity is hard to capture:

> Even from the balcony, however, people who lead never get an objective picture because they never entirely dispense with the filters through which they perceive events. Nor can they learn about their own filters and biases and factor them into their interpretations. (Heifetz, 1994, p. 271)

Leaning on partners (confidants and allies) and intentionally spending time in reflection help me to see clearly (or as clearly as I can). This requires that you have default positions that are the opposite of what people generally think of when they think of strong leaders. What are your starting points when you think about solving problems and helping your college to move forward? Is your default certainty that you are right within a closed system of logic? Or, is it uncertainty within an open system of logic? Do you assume that you have all of the necessary information? Or do you assume that you are missing something that someone else can help you with? Do you assume that you are right, and that you are seeing clearly? Or do you leave open the possibility that you are wrong, and someone can help you? To admit and operate on the premise that you don't know everything and that you don't see all issues in objective terms and that you need help—takes courage, humility, and the willingness to be vulnerable. Having these as your default positions represents a leadership strength, not a weakness.

Find a Sanctuary

> Listening to oneself requires a place where one can hear oneself think ... To exercise leadership, one has to expect to get swept up in the music. One has to plan for it and develop scheduled opportunities that anticipate the need to regain perspective. (Heifetz, 1994, p. 273)

There was a series of articles in the Chronicle of Higher Education in the spring of 2018 that looked at different aspects of being a college dean. There were articles on attracting talented people to the position (Anft, 2018) and advice for people who were considering a move to administration. One of the articles highlighted people's perspective of you once you become dean. I think this was less pronounced for me because I was an external candidate, but it was still there. It's the idea that no matter how you see yourself—dean, professor, or some combination of the two—people will see you as the dean (Perlmutter, 2018). With this role firmly surrounding you and everything you do, how people interact with you informs how you interact with them and how they see the decisions you make. And, decision making is the aspect of this job that separates it from any other job I've had. As chair and director and professor, there is almost always someone above you on the organizational chart who makes the final call on decisions. As dean, there are many things that I don't decide, per se, but instead recommend to the provost and president. However, there are many things that are left to me to decide. The weight of making decisions can get to you over time.

My outlook on this is that you build trust with the people that surround you, collect as much information as possible to inform your thinking, start with the entire college in mind, and make decisions that you think are right. What decision is best for the most number of people? I found that keeping the big picture in mind helped me navigate decision-making and the questions that I faced after I made these decisions. Is there a chance that you have made the wrong decision? Of course. But that's a possibility regardless of your decision-making process.

Finding a sanctuary amid this process is fundamental to the work of being a dean, just as it was when I was a middle school teacher. The work is and can be all consuming. I need to do things that are completely unrelated to my role as leader of the college. The first thing that I do is disconnect from screens—iPhone and computers—on a regular basis. As I have already mentioned (Chapter 1), I don't check or send email after 5:00 p.m. on weekdays and sporadically (if at all) on the weekends. This is an intentional effort to draw a line between work time and personal time—for me and the people with whom I work. There is no need for people to be on call 24/7. Finding my sanctuary is a part of my morning routine—writing, meditation, and exercise. Anything that gets me out of dean mode and into any other kind of existence is a sanctuary for me—going for a walk around campus to get out of the office, cooking dinner after a stressful day, playing cards, talking with my wife, and my personal favorite, making a campfire in the backyard with my son.

Preserve a Sense of Purpose

Leadership oftentimes is a passionate and consuming activity. People need inspiration and drive to step out into a void which only later is recognized as a place of creativity and development. (Heifetz, 1994, p. 274)

Leading a college, as the quote above alludes to, can be all consuming. The first year of serving as dean has been some of the most rewarding work that I have ever had the privilege of doing. It has also been some of the most difficult work that I have done. As the spring semester ended, I could feel the physical toll that the work was taking on me. In the academic year cycle, late spring is known for being the time of year when everyone is tired and ready for the year to wrap up. When I was a middle school teacher/coach and when I was a faculty member, I could always sense these feelings around the middle of April and into May. It was an indication that you had put in an honest effort and that the year was almost complete. It is a time for celebration and rite of passage for graduates. The pomp and circumstance of the ritual signifying the end of another year. I couldn't help but notice how the feelings of fatigue were more pronounced and heightened. I was exhausted. The reason is simple. After a year of meeting new people, building new degree programs, improving systems within the college, and doing a myriad of other things that had never been done before, the work had caught up with me. These feelings were tempered and bolstered by a sense that we, the college, had worked hard and accomplished the things we set out to accomplish. Tired, yes. But, mostly I was proud of the people in the college and the work that we had done.

For me, my sense of purpose has three sources. It's these three sources that serve to sustain me in the difficult and important work we are here to do. The first two have always been a part of my professional identity, and the third one I have developed during my first year as dean.

First, my sense of purpose as an educator is defined and sustained by the memory of teachers who have helped me along my journey. The sense of purpose that my elementary, middle, and high school teachers had is with me always. The teachers I had the privilege of learning from, the coaches that taught me lessons in the context of sports, the professors that showed me different ways to see the world—all inform my sense of purpose. These lessons and experiences did not begin and end with me. I was just the next link in the chain. A chain that I am now a part of: my second grade teacher, Ms. Estes, who taught me that it was okay to mess up; my eighth grade algebra teacher, Ms. Craig, who taught me about perspective and how to change my mind about things I thought I "wasn't good at"; my ninth grade English teacher, Ms. Morrow, who taught me that writing, as an act of expression, takes a measure of courage; my football coach, Coach Green, who taught me how to win with class and lose with honor. These are just a few of the people that fuel my sense of purpose and who serve to represent parts of the mosaic of who I am as a person. That is the power of the profession of teaching, and that is why I am honored to do what I do. Teaching and teachers matter because we are all composites of the people who teach us important lessons along the way. They are a part of who we eventually become. For these people, I am eternally grateful.

Second, I am sustained by my belief in public education as a common good. Not a private, for profit good—a public good. I am proud to be a part of public education in the United States. And, yes. I know that there is enough bad press to go around about our profession, and it's mostly engineered and proliferated by powerful groups that want to privatize education and/or make it into another commodity that is sold in the "free market." Attempts to measure what teachers do and the effort to make every aspect of the job into a marketable skill that is "practical" are harming the efforts of teaching (as a profession) to get a fair hearing. People who are in education know this. As I was writing this chapter, teachers in Oklahoma, West Virginia, and Kentucky were on strike to push back against unreasonable working conditions and low pay. I am proud to call these teachers and public servants my colleagues.

Another aspect of public education bears noting. One of the original justifications for taxpayer funded public education was to educate every child so that they might sustain the American experiment in democracy. This isn't just in social studies where this sentiment is more explicit. The purpose of public education is to educate children to be members of our democratic society, not a worker who can "compete in the 21st century economy" (whatever that means). Of course, we want people to be able to find work in whatever century they happen to live, but is that the primary purpose of an education? I don't think so. And, who is so arrogant to assume that you will know what the world economy will look like in 20 years? I don't think that Ms. Estes and Ms. Craig and Ms. Morrow and Coach Green were overly concerned about my possible employment or whether I could "compete in the global economy." Teachers don't control the global economy. Let's stop pretending that the man or woman who teaches fourth grade has any bearing on global markets or the skills that will be required when their students are in their mid-twenties. That's not how it works. Anyone who has worked with children in a classroom knows this. Teachers are called to a higher ideal. Higher than isolated skills for some future day when their children are working adults. They are about more than helping students to find employment. They are concerned about helping children grow into adults who can navigate and thrive in this world, and I am proud to be a part of this tradition.

Third, I find purpose in the history of my current institution. Back in the fall, I was reading Sample's (2002) *Contrarian's Guide to Leadership*. He writes about the power of origin stories, those stories that help us understand our history and where we came from as an institution. At the time, I can remember asking myself: Outside of the information on the college website about the history of my current institution, what did I know about the history of my new institution? The answer: not much. The next day, I went to our library and checked out two books on the history of my new institution, and over the next week or so, decided to learn about our history. What I learned has been a part of my sense of purpose during my first year as dean. The history that I learned from these two books (Gildrie &

Winn, 2002; Waters, 1977) forms a foundational part of how I talk about our institution. One of the great things about being a college dean is that you are asked to speak to groups of people on a pretty regular basis. This history is always a part of what I have to say because it connects what we are doing now to the people who founded our university. Paying attention to this history forms a common link between the caring, dedicated worldview of our founders and the caring, dedicated worldview of the current faculty and staff, and most importantly, the graduates that we produce. What does our shared history tell us? Below are a few of the highlights that I share with people every chance I get.

- Our university was founded by public school teachers and administrators.
- The stated purpose of our university (in the beginning) was to train teachers for the rural public schools of the state.
- The first two students to enroll came from working class families looking to better their lives.
- The first class had 158 students, and tuition, room, board, and student fees (combined) would cost you $66.
- The first faculty consisted of seven men and nine women—all but one had been teachers and administrators in public schools.
- A statement from the first catalog (1930) reveals how the profession of teaching and the effort of teachers are the reason that we have a university today:

The Austin Peay Normal School is not just another state teachers college. It occupies a unique place among the teacher training institutions of the state. It directs its major energies toward and centers its chief activities about the education and training of prospective teachers and teachers in service for the elementary schools of Tennessee. This means something. It means...better training of teachers for our schools. (as cited in Waters, 1977, p. 52)

In the span of our institution's history, we have transformed from 158 students to more than 10,000. We have gone from being a normal (teacher training) school, to a regional, comprehensive university, offering associates degrees through doctorates. We started with 16 faculty, and now we have more than 300. We started with students from Tennessee and the surrounding states, and now we serve students from Tennessee and over 30 countries. We serve and educate students to a level that our founders couldn't have imagined. We are a part of this legacy; it is something that should sustain our sense of purpose.

And, it all started with teachers on a mission to educate children. That's our past, present, and future.

Final Thoughts

> *Behind the mountains, there are more mountains.*
> —Haitian Proverb

As a writer, I have always found it difficult to write conclusions. When I wrote my dissertation in graduate school, I am pretty sure I wrote five drafts of the conclusion. It's hard to wrap it up, and tie a bow on a project as if it's finished. I found the same to be true with this book. I am writing this at 5:15 on the morning of June 15th, two weeks before the one-year mark of being a rookie dean. As I sit here, I have to replace my very capable associate dean (who left for another opportunity). I am waiting on a phone call for final approval on an academic program from our regional accreditor. I will be interviewing two candidates for an open position to replace one of our retired literacy faculty. I am slated to speak with an external education group about how we have developed our partnerships with the local schools so they can write a case study about our college. I am meeting with a senior faculty member about revisions to our retention, promotion, and tenure guidelines. I have a call placed to our university lawyers about a student situation. These are things that are on my calendar to do. Today. So, it's hard to think, much less write, in ways that suggest that I am at an ending or that anything is finished. The arbitrary one-year date is closing in, but it is clear that nothing is concluding. It's in progress.

Being a first year dean is like standing on the beach. Growing up in Alabama, one of the few places that we ever got to go on vacation was the beach. As a child I can remember the power of the waves, as they would pull me in to the gulf, only to have them crash and push me back towards the shore. The push and pull, push and pull, push and pull. Most waves you could see coming, but occasionally a big one would hit you. These didn't push you back towards the shore. The bigger ones crush you under their weigh and roll you on the bottom of the surf. You might get injured in these cases. For a brief moment, it can be pretty scary. Having your body tossed and thrown against the bottom of the ocean. You swallow salt water as your shoulders and head bounce off of the ocean floor, as your body is washed up. I have watched my son engage in this same exercise. He walks out into the water. He times his jumps to float over the waves. But, once in a while a big one gets him, and he goes under. In a few seconds he pops up, recovers, and goes back out. He goes back out. As a dean, you have to go back out.

Most days are like most waves. You see them coming. You check your calendar for your appointments, make mental notes and adjustments, take advice from your leadership team, and you jump. Most of the time you make it over the day/wave. Sometimes you don't. This is normal. Just get back up. This won't be the last big wave you see. Once you are back on your feet, and after the rhythms of the day/week/month are restored you will notice that the big wave that rolled you wasn't as bad as it seemed in the moment. It never is. Sitting in the dean's chair you come to realize that things are rarely as good or bad as they seem. And, you realize that another big wave will come. Eventually.

It is important to remember that what you stand for, as a human being, matters more than technical skills. When you first start out you will be ignorant of the technical know how required to be a dean. There are systems that are a part of the university that you won't know how to use, reports that you won't know how to access (or read), state and federal agencies that you won't know about, and regulations and policies that are new to you. All this is normal. You will learn these things over time. It seems that these are more important than what they really are (Yes. They *are* important). I think this is the case because much of the information flow and requests for your attention derives from these external sources. When a request is made, and we don't know, we feel stupid. You're not stupid; you are ignorant of a system that is specific to this college or university. In fact, everyone at your institution will feel the same way you do in a couple years when the university decides to change the system and go with another vendor (literally happens all the time). So, relax on this.

It's more important that you stand for something and that you are an ethical human being. One of my favorite quotes from the Stoic philosopher Marcus Aurelius is, "What is your vocation? To be a good person" (Holliday & Hanselman, 2016, p. 165). The people that follow you deserve a leader that tries to be a good human being. Not a perfect human being, but an ethical person who chooses good.

Last, remember that it's going to be alright. This is one of my life mantras. I would often say this to people I met with who were having a problem or issue in their area. It's usually the first thing I say to people after they tell me about their troubles. They tell me what's going on, dumping an inordinate amount of information for me (and them) to process. They lean back in their chair, and take a deep breath, wanting me to make a comment or offer a solution. This is what I usually say, "it's going to be alright." I say this because it's true. There are very few emergencies in the line of work that we are privileged to do. It helps everyone involved to see things as fixable, non-emergencies, that can be made right. Because almost, almost everything can be fixed. Almost everything can be made right. On my worst days, my advisers would tell me the same thing, and I could hear my words being said back to me.

Saying it's going to be alright works because it's true and people intuitively know it. They just need a reminder. Our actions follow our words and thoughts. Let these be your words. We say this. We believe this. We solve problems. We solve problems because our default positions are not set in stone. They are malleable and changeable. It's a choice we make, like most of the aspects of being a dean. They are choices we make. Let's choose good and right and cooperation and transparency and optimism and love. They are better than the alternatives.

References

Anft, M. (2018). No one wants to be your dean. *Chronicle of Higher Education, 64*(32), 8–11.

Comey, J. (2018). *A higher loyalty: Truth, lies, and leadership.* New York, NY: Flatiron Books.

Gildrie, R., & Winn, T. (2002). *A history of Austin Peay State University 1927–2002: And its predecessors, 1806–1926.* Clarksville, TN: Austin Peay State University.

Heifetz, R. (1994). *Leadership without easy answers.* Cambridge, MA: Harvard University Press.

Holliday, R., & Hanselman, S. (2016). *The daily stoic: 366 meditations on wisdom, perseverance, and the art of living.* New York, NY: Portfolio.

Palmer, P. (2017). *The courage to teach: Exploring the inner landscape of a teacher's life.* San Francisco, CA: Jossey-Bass.

Perlmutter, D. (2018). How to be both a professor and a dean. *Chronicle of Higher Education, 64*(32), 11–12.

Sample, S. (2002). *Contrarian's Guide to Leadership.* San Francisco, CA: Jossey-Bass.

Waters, C.M. (1977). *The first fifty years of Austin Peay State University.* Clarksville, TN: Austin Peay State University.

If

by Rudyard Kipling

If you can keep your head when all about you
    Are losing theirs and blaming it on you,

If you can trust yourself when all men doubt you,
    But make allowance for their doubting too;

If you can wait and not be tired by waiting,
    Or being lied about, don't deal in lies,

Or being hated, don't give way to hating,
    And yet don't look too good, nor talk too wise:

If you can dream—and not make dreams your master;
    If you can think—and not make thoughts your aim;

If you can meet with Triumph and Disaster
    And treat those two impostors just the same;

If you can bear to hear the truth you've spoken
    Twisted by knaves to make a trap for fools,

Or watch the things you gave your life to, broken,
    And stoop and build 'em up with worn-out tools:

If you can make one heap of all your winnings
    And risk it on one turn of pitch-and-toss,

And lose, and start again at your beginnings
    And never breathe a word about your loss;

If you can force your heart and nerve and sinew
    To serve your turn long after they are gone,

And so hold on when there is nothing in you
    Except the Will which says to them: 'Hold on!'

If you can talk with crowds and keep your virtue,
　Or walk with Kings—nor lose the common touch,

If neither foes nor loving friends can hurt you,
　If all men count with you, but none too much;

If you can fill the unforgiving minute
　With sixty seconds' worth of distance run,

Yours is the Earth and everything that's in it,
　And—which is more—you'll be a Man, my son!

Acknowledgments

Examples of leadership are everywhere. We just have to look around. My entire life, I have been surrounded by leaders—in my family, in schools, on the sports field, and now in higher education. What little I know about leadership, I have picked up from these special people.

Thank you...

To the first leaders I was able to observe and learn from, my parents. Thanks for setting good examples for my sisters and me.

To my mentor, Dr. Amanda Branscombe, for always being there to listen.

To my teachers and coaches who were the embodiment of leadership.

To Kim Mauldin, who helped a lost freshman get registered for classes in the fall of 1997.

To my editors, Tiffany Dolder-Holland and Lisa Barron, for reading drafts of this book and providing much needed feedback.

To the faculty and staff at three universities (Athens State University, University of Cincinnati, and Austin Peay State University) for allowing me to learn with and from you.

To The Dean's Council, Lisa Barron, Benita Bruster, Theresa Dezellem, Moniqueka Gold, Jana Hatcher, and John McConnell for helping me to lead the college.

And, to my wife Kristen, whom I love more every day, for her support and willingness to help me think through the next idea I have.

About the Author

Dr. Prentice Chandler is Dean and Professor of the Eriksson College of Education at Austin Peay State University in Clarksville (TN). From 2013–2017, he was the Associate Director of Teacher Education and Leadership and an Associate Professor of Social Studies Education at the University of Cincinnati (OH). Prior to his time at Cincinnati, he was the Department Chair of Secondary Education and an Associate/Assistant Professor of History and Social Science Education at Athens State University (AL). Before joining the professoriate, Dr. Chandler taught middle and high school social studies at Clements High School in Limestone County (AL). He also taught in the geography department at the University of North Alabama as an adjunct from 2002–2005.

Dr. Chandler's scholarship and writing interests are in the areas of history and social studies education, critical race theory, academic freedom, and authentic intellectual work. Dr. Chandler has authored or coauthored approximately 50 works, including two books on teaching about race and racism within the social studies curriculum. In 2007, Dr. Chandler was awarded the *Defense of Academic Freedom Award* from the National Council for the Social Studies (NCSS) for his efforts teaching history in Alabama public schools. In 2018, he was awarded the *Notable Leader in Teacher Education Award* from the Alabama Association of Teacher Educators.

CPSIA information can be obtained
at www.ICGtesting.com
Printed in the USA
LVHW082014280619
622706LV00003B/12/P